Happiness
in the
21st Century

MANUEL SIERRA JIMENEZ

authorHOUSE®

AuthorHouse™ UK
1663 Liberty Drive
Bloomington, IN 47403 USA
www.authorhouse.co.uk
Phone: UK TFN: 0800 0148641 (Toll Free inside the UK)
*   UK Local: 02036 956322 (+44 20 3695 6322 from outside the UK)*

Published by AuthorHouse 01/29/2021

ISBN: 978-1-6655-8479-1 (sc)
ISBN: 978-1-6655-8480-7 (e)

Print information available on the last page.

Contents

Acknowledgements

In this section I would like to thank all the people who have helped me directly or indirectly in the making of this book. It has taken almost four years of reading, researching, organizing and structuring to be able to bring this longed-for project to fruition. It has been a complicated task for me. In fact, a real challenge. In truth, I have been tempted, at times, to give up writing and also, I admit, to finish the book in an inadequate way, because of my impatience. I would like to think that I have achieved my goal: that of communicating my life experience to my potential readers, always with the aim of being able to guide others on how to become happier. Due to my initial inexperience, this undertaking would not have been possible if it were not for the constant support of my family and friends. They have been a great help both technically and morally because at no time have they stopped encouraging me, correcting me, making observations and suggestions. They have made me consider other aspects, issues that I had not been aware of. Then I came up with new ideas and relationships which linked the contents. Thanks, I repeat, to these people I have been able to continue the work as well as enrich and improve it. For this reason I would like to mention the following names. Thanks to their collaboration "HAPPINESS IN THE 21st CENTURY; Guide for a Full Life" has been able to see the light, in the way it has done today. To my wife Lois and to my family: to my mother Juana María, to my sister Isabel María, to my uncle Braulio and to my nieces for their great emotional support. To my friends: Timothy, Alicia and Peter for providing me with their valuable experience to exemplify some issues. To my friends Antonio Rosselló and Jaime Obrador Antúnez for having helped me find my own way and being a reference for me. To the interviewees: Toni Estelrich Mesquida, Salvador Vidal Jaume, Apol·lònia Monserrat Obrador and David Medina i Bombardó for their collaboration. To the publishing house: for having trusted in the results that the printing and diffusion of this first work may have, and especially to Bernat Estelrich Mesquida and Marta Aspachs Pagès for the correction and follow-up of the writing of the book.

Preface

Some may wonder why I had the idea of writing a book of this nature when other authors had already undertaken something similar. Who hasn't ever thought about improving their life, being happier or achieving a more or less permanent state of happiness? There are many writers that have tried, with greater or lesser success, to respond to this dream of the human being. In this sense I have wanted to contribute my grain of sand, relying on my life experience and my reading, giving the question a more practical and interactive approach. If you really want to improve your life and be happy, "HAPPINESS IN THE 21st CENTURY; Guide for a Full Life" can help you since you will not only read it but also interact with it through the many exercises and reflective situations that will be proposed to you throughout the work. Many years have passed since then, but it can be said that the seed of this book was already sown in my childhood. Although I only lived in Orellana La Vieja (Badajoz) in Spain for my first four years of life, the truth is that I can remember an extraordinary event that happened to me there. Due to an accident caused by one of the pigs my parents kept in a neighbouring field, I became paralysed, unable to walk at all. At the San Rafael hospital in Madrid, the doctors advised my family that I should have an operation, but fortune or destiny urged them to take me back to the village, to the Monastery of Guadalupe to pray to the Virgin for the success of the operation. In response to our devotion, I inexplicably began to walk again, little by little, after only a short time. The doctors decided that it was no longer necessary for me to go to the operating theatre as I had been cured. Each of you can reflect on what this extraordinary healing was about. It depends on your beliefs but for me, this event, although I was very young, had a lasting impact on me. Soon after, we all moved to Felanitx, a town in the south of Mallorca (Balearic Islands). There my parents hoped to find work and give my sister and me a future. I started my studies at the San Alfonso School, in the same town. From those first years I remember that I had to adapt to a very different place. On many occasions, people who came from outside were marginalised, making it harder - and more painful – to secure employment and earn a living. "Outsiders", as we were called by the natives of the island, were not of the same class, so to speak. In adolescence these social differences became more evident. Luckily, while I had to deal with a somewhat hostile environment, I met some very special people: my first friends. I have to thank especially Antoni Rosselló who, at the age of 13, introduced me to the world of chess. With him I learned to play and also to compete as part of the team of Felanitx, which was already in a top category. All this helped me to feel valued and appreciated during those difficult years. At the age of 16 I started attending yoga classes. My first teacher was Jaume, who also happened to be a physical education teacher at the Colegio de San Alfonso. This discipline gave me character, security, mental control and also the satisfaction of being part of a team and group. Along with chess, yoga would become the other pillar of my life, which would later link me to Buddhism and Eastern wisdom. However, interest in this culture had already been awakened in me long before, when, at the age of only 7, I was attracted to the monks of Tibet. I was intrigued and amazed by their exotic origins and their calm, happy faces. In my teenage years, strong concerns arose in me. I asked myself things like: Who am I really? Why does humanity behave as it does? Why are there very rich people and others who can barely find enough to eat every day? Why doesn't everybody always do good in their life? Why are there so many conflicts and wars in the world? What can - and must - I do to be well and to improve myself every day? At this time I read books on self-help, philosophy and yoga. I was especially struck by: "*The Integral Yoga*" by Sri Aurobindo, "*Metaphysical Meditations*" by Descartes and the self-help book; "*Heaven is the Limit*". These works produced a deep and radical change within me. They gave me clarity of mind, and made me pay more attention to my thoughts, my soul and my being. When I look back on those years, I see in me a sensitive and insecure boy, who felt somewhat marginalized, and who thanks to good friends and the discovery of chess and yoga, was able to mature and grow.

In this way I was always trying to help fellow students, who, without having my own strength as back-up for them, were also suffering from some kind of discrimination. If I look back, I now remember a young man who was educated, kind and always willing to help. I don't want to end this stage of life without mentioning my friend Guillermo. He was a neighbour, an older man who had no children or family around and was quite lonely. In spite of the age difference we connected and became very close friends. Seen from a distance I think we learned a lot from each other. It was an enriching relationship, a great example if we think that nowadays there is great neglect, and even rejection, of older people. In my adolescence I felt different from others. My concerns, although largely satisfied by my devotion to self-help reading, did not prevent me from being very sensitive to everything around me. So from the beginning my attitude was to treat people with respect, politeness and courtesy, exactly as I would like to be treated. All humans are equal. We are first and foremost people. No one is above or below anyone else in terms of their status as a human being. No matter what religion, background, habitat, social or family status, we all have the right to be happy. Each of us chooses the exact moment when we decide to change and improve our lives and start looking towards the future.to improve ourselves in everything. Later on I studied Business management and office studies at the Institute in the same town. At the age of 17 I was already working in the hotel business as a waiter in Calas de Mallorca. I continued for many years in that industry, later as a Sector Manager, and finally as Restaurant Manager. I have always balanced this work with studies in Buddhism, yoga and psychology. As I had to travel to do these courses and workshops, I got to know different cities, people of different classes and characters. When I was 22 years old I attended some talks at the Buddhist Centre of Palma de Mallorca, in Morey Street. The classes were given by monks from Tibet. This experience was extremely important for me. At last I found people who understood me, who gave me answers, and who, in the end, practised a philosophy completely similar to mine. I felt at home there. The monks and their companions became like a second family to me. So I decided to become a Buddhist. When the monks came to Mallorca I nearly always attended their seminars and conferences. I listened to their teachings and philosophy and tried to follow the practices. I continued to read books on mind control, self-help and yoga. One thing led to another and I ended up becoming a vegetarian. After a while I decided to take a course in Yoga teaching. Curiously, I have only taught this discipline on a few occasions and only to small groups of friends. Not everyone is prepared for the doctrine which underpins the study of yoga. That was a very active time in my life. I travelled a lot to Madrid and Barcelona. I was constantly attending courses and seminars. My restless nature was like a non-stop engine. However, it was not until a few years ago that I had the idea of writing something serious and well-founded in order to motivate and advise people. A few years had already passed since the first questions I posed as a teenager. I had travelled through Germany, Russia, France, England, Spain and Portugal and despite having lived through different experiences and met people from all walks of life, I was not used to one thing: seeing people unhappy. In many places, in my comings and goings, I observed men and women, in the metro, in the cinema, in parks, in hotels, in shops... their faces did not reflect the happiness and peace of mind that a person can express when they are content with life. However, the spark or trigger for writing this book came after meeting a couple in Bristol: Timothy and Alice. He was 34 years old.

He was thin, with a small beard, athletic, and dark-skinned. His parents were from India, but he had been born in the Rusholme district of Manchester, which is often called "the curry mile" due to the large number of Indian restaurants in the area. He had lived for many years in Norman Street, near Birchfields Park, and had studied at the grammar school. Although he was still young, he was already very interested in helping out in his parents' business. They had an Indian food distribution chain that supplied different Indian food restaurants. However, for young Timothy, this was not what he had in mind for his future. He dreamed of having his own business one day. So he prepared himself well and studied "Economics Management" at Oxford.

His partner, Alicia, had already turned 32. She was blonde, tall, with a youthful, serene appearance. She was born in Holland Park and spent her childhood in Queensway Street, on the outskirts of London. This neighbourhood is popular for its markets and buildings with their origins in Mediaeval times. At Hallfield Primary School, she excelled academically. Later she studied psychology at King's College London. Her parents were Russian, they had a clothing shop in Leicester Square in London. I met Timothy and Alice at a party in one of their pubs in Bristol. We immediately connected and talked about hospitality. It was a subject I knew well as I had always worked in tourism-related centres. After this meeting, we became very friendly, and I advised them, from time to time, on how to run their business. It didn't take me long to realise something. Even though they apparently had everything - money, health and friends, deep down they were not happy. In fact, over time, they came to tell me about some of their little problems. To be honest, I could see it coming. They both spent a lot of time managing business in pubs, where they had to place orders with distributors. The couple eventually separated, at least for some time, and the management of the pubs was divided up. In spite of everything, I kept in touch with them. Once, after going out to dinner with Timothy, I recommended the following: I asked him why he didn't tone down the degree to which he was involved in pub management - maybe this way he would have more time for his personal life and could perhaps save his marriage. At first he was very reluctant to accept my advice. He told me, however, that he would think about it. Perhaps I insisted a little more than was necessary. I made him see that his two small children needed him more than anything else in life and that this would give him more time to be with them. The thing, then, was a bit up in the air. After a few weeks, Timothy called me. He wanted to see me and I thought he had something important to tell me. I found him a bit nervous, and his voice was a bit higher than usual. I immediately thought that something was not quite right, and we arranged to meet in the afternoon. Once in the park, he explained to me that he couldn't continue with this inner discomfort and would follow my advice. He would move two of the pubs from his responsibility, and stay with just one. He came to an agreement with the managers of the establishment so that he could save his marriage, and he would return to Alicia and the two little ones, or at least he would try to do so. I was completely surprised. I could not believe it. Timothy had listened to me and had decided to follow my advice. I thought it was wonderful that someone had decided to rebuild his life by giving up money, or at least a large part of it, but above all that he had listened to me and reacted. This fact made me think that just as I helped them, I could also help many other people to be happy. I just had to find a way to reach them, and offer them the opportunity to be happy, no matter where they live, who they are or what they work as. Being happy depends on us, on our way of approaching our life. Not on the outside. That is how I decided to write this book. A conversation with a friend meant opening Pandora's box for me. It was the inspiration to start this work. I helped Timothy but he helped me, without realizing it, much more. Manuel Sierra Jiménez Bristol, August 2018.

Introduction

The fact that you have acquired this book may indicate that you are quite interested in your happiness. If you feel unsatisfied or not happy at all "HAPPINESS IN THE 21st CENTURY; Guide for a Full Life" can help you achieve it. Reading its contents and exercises will fill you with positive energy and bring out genuinely uplifting thoughts. This guide to your happiness is intended to do nothing more than to "awaken" the impulse to improve, whatever your starting point may be. If the reader can place himself – or herself - at this point, it will mean that we are on the right track, and that I have contributed something in guiding them towards a more real, fuller and more fruitful existence. The chapters are arranged so that the reader can understand progressively, step by step, and grasp the overall idea of the meaning of the work. They will all lead you to a degree of commitment to yourself, and promote inner harmony, permanent enthusiasm and joy. A proper reading of this work can make you a more fulfilled human being, dedicated to a life in all its completeness. The work of framing reflections and advice is a meticulous and complex task, always determined by a certain limited subjectivism. Nevertheless, the classification of the chapters alternated with the practical exercises will,

I believe, make it more suggestive and enjoyable to read. Throughout the book you will find exercises and reflections that – if you work deeply on them - can be transformed into elevated and effective messages. In this way you will have the tools to achieve a more positive change in your life. At first you may feel that some contents are repeated throughout the book, so don't let it bore you. The book has been structured in such a way that it connects with each theme as a whole. Each section begins with a synthesis of what has already been seen, to which new information is added. The reader can thus become better acquainted with both theory and practice. This novel work has been made more enjoyable by four interviews, testimonies of people who are very different from each other, which illustrate one of the themes that concerns humanity most: achieving happiness. I will give a small example, to start the path to happiness. Imagine you are the conductor of a large philharmonic orchestra and you are in the middle of a concert. In this imaginary scenario, the concert would become your life, while the musicians would represent the daily situations you encounter.

A good conductor gets all the musicians to play in unison and in harmony with the rhythms and musical interpretation which he determines. The conductor, in this case, would be his inner self. This book is not what is meant by a self-help book. In this sense my purpose is somewhat more ambitious, as it wants to go one step further. By this I want to stress that I personally have nothing against this kind of reading. In my adolescent years I read a great deal of these texts and they were of great help to me at the time. In short, this work aims to guide you to help yourself but within a gradual personal development that you will assume step by step. To this end I have introduced work exercises, reflections and ideas that will make you think and ask yourself transcendental questions. Following this path requires optimism and self-encouragement. For this first stage I will suggest many practical exercises. Please, do not limit yourself to reading this book "from a distance" as if it were a novel. Read slowly, take your time, and try to get the best out of each chapter. Learn to read between the lines, if you need to read it three times, that's so much better than just once. Participate. Reading should be interactive to be more effective. To start with, we should acquire a greater awareness of ourselves, of our present situation. Then it will be important to organize a simple plan to overcome initial inertia whereby we want to remain in our "comfort zone". This comfort zone slyly beckons us to stay in the places we are accustomed to, adopting the same habits, preferring to live in a simple way, without risking further complications in life. What I am proposing is not a solution to everything, but rather a suggested method to learn how to manage the problems that arise. With a few simple exercises, we will achieve a healthier way of living that will help us feel better, and become more aware of the world around us. You will learn to minimize the daily inconveniences of this new approach to life, and also something very important - to take advantage of them. If you take the initiative to try a healthier way of living, it shows that you have understood that with each new challenge – and resolution of those challenges – the greater will be your ability to achieve a life of true quality. To be well, to be happy, is easier than you imagine. I am not saying that it is totally easy and requires no soul-searching, but not as complicated as many people visualise it to be – as a long, never-ending journey towards uncertainty. We have to be really sure of what we want to achieve to be happy; or from another point of view, be sure of the things we really don't need to be happy. You will be able to focus on: ▸ High personal motivation. ▸ Having more friends. ▸ Securing your wishes and desires in life. ▸ Changing and renewing yourself. ▸ Enjoying things more, including family life. ▸ Improving your sense of humour. ▸ Living the life you always wanted to live. ▸ Improving yourself in almost every way including mental and emotional control. ▸ Bringing insecurity to an end ▸ Enjoying more of every day, hour, minute, second of your existence.

It is important to know where we stand, to know where the north and south are in our lives. To know where we are and where we are going. In short, to know what the real objectives are that we want to achieve. "Happiness in the 21st century" will show you the way, as it combines characteristics of rigour, motivation and energy. The first step is to approach all the things we do and almost everything that happens to us with enthusiasm. Get up in the morning, take a deep breath, smile at life, and give life thanks for giving us the wonderful opportunity to exist in the here and now. Life is full of fine possibilities. We just have to open our eyes and be aware of everything that is happening around us and how it can act in our favour. Let us place ourselves in immediate present, at "zero" hour and "zero" minute. Let's make a realistic assessment of our path. It is never too late to change. The first phase you will involve you learning to have daily optimism, and little by little you will become accustomed to it. In general we may know many things about the operation and maintenance of our cars (for example) but surprisingly very little about taking care of our own body, and mind. In most cases, practical knowledge alone is not enough to achieve happiness. Our lifestyle has a great influence on our state of mind. It is striking that while the vast majority of people desperately seek happiness, few find it. Almost all of us have a fairly reasonable understanding of what happiness is, so why is it that some have such a long way to go that very few achieve it? In short, "Happiness in the 21st Century" is meant to be a workbook, not a simple reading. With this I want to emphasize that it is important that the reader heeds the recommendations and advice, but above all he should do some simple exercises.

This is a practical book that will bring you great benefits every day. From this moment on I invite you to start the journey towards happiness. I will accompany you on this journey from now on. Together we will walk and not only reach our destination but learn from it, filling your whole being with harmony, and your mind with great understanding and clarity.

Chapter 1

The idea of happiness

If we ask "what happiness is" we probably do not find it easy to define. It will be easier to use words with a similar meaning which will help us to describe what it is that we want to convey when we need to describe "what it is to be happy", "to feel well", "to feel joy" and "to be satisfied". In general, all these are expressions that serve to represent states that people feel when we achieve a desired goal. Happiness would therefore be an internal and subjective emotion. The person would experience it in relation to a certain external fact, but it would have more to do with the attitude with which that event is experienced. What for some individuals is a motive for happiness and contentment, for others, this might not be the case or may even mean misfortune and depression.

If, from one person to another, the attainment of happiness can mean something very different, let us imagine how this concept has travelled through history. If we take a look at our origins as rational humans and compare them with

1

today's societies, interesting aspects can be observed. This can help us better understand our current way of living and the current concept of happiness.

Our lifestyle

Thousands of years ago, in general, people lived for an average of between thirty and forty years. It was not until the Industrial Revolution that hygiene measures were introduced to protect health. Together with these, advances in medicine significantly increased the life expectancy of the population at birth. Today, we live about forty years longer. Our ancestors had to fight hard to survive, having to face all manner of challenges, e.g. sudden changes of weather on a global scale leading to glaciation or melting ice, falling meteorites, earthquakes, volcanic eruptions, dangerous animals, disease, food shortages and warring between clans over survival resources. The path of humanity has not always been easy.

At that time, people were more concerned with subsistence and staying alive than with happiness. Being so focused on finding food and shelter left them little time for the luxury of considering whether they were really happy or not, and indeed, how would they have defined such a concept within the framework of their own lives? As time wore on, a nomadic lifestyle gave way to a settled existence associated with farming and land ownership. Our ancestors learned to cultivate the land, and so began agriculture and the rearing of livestock. At that stage, people no longer needed to go hunting and fishing every day in order to be able to eat.

With this new approach to life, food production increased; life became less uncertain and safer. People learned to store what they could not consume and thus had the security of an all-year-round supply of food. These developments may seem simple or trivial to many of us, but they were really important for the essential well-being of our ancestors. It could have been during this massive leap in societal development, after their primary needs had been secured, that people found time and capacity to devote to thinking "what is it that I want?" and "what is it that makes me feel?" this sensation of what today we know as "happiness".

Thus, during the Neolithic period, with the establishment of agriculture and livestock rearing, an economic development food place, which had not been seen before in the history of humanity arrived, i.e. a surplus of production. That is to say, when the weather was good and the harvests were abundant, not only could food be stored for winter or times of scarcity but our ancestors came to accumulate excess produce. Hence, the market place heralded exchange of food, clothing, crafts and livestock, i.e. a system which would later come to be known as "bartering".

Even though coins were not yet used for primitive trade, a process began whereby some population groups differed from others owing to different levels of economic stability. The equality that had existed in the ancient clans of the Palaeolithic and Mesolithic age began to fade. Now, some had more than others. Economic status and greater wealth generated the first social differences. For those who had more, this meant being able to lead more qualitative lives and a greater chance for peace. The less fortunate were those who possessed the least. The settling down of these first peoples into stable populations also helped to shape a new pattern of organisation of labour.

Originating from the different agricultural livestock activities, the first trades arose and with them, societal differences increased. From a totally communitarian system, a more orderly and hierarchical organisation developed where each individual had a position or a job, e.g. the blacksmith, the basket maker or the bread maker, amongst others.

The modern lifestyle we know today is actually not that old. Society underwent a great change after the first Industrial Revolution. This process of economic, social and technological transformation began in the second half of the 18th century in England. A few decades later, it would spread to much of Western Europe and North America, reaching a plateau between 1820 and 1840.

This period saw the greatest set of economic, technological and social transformations of humanity since the Neolithic era. Rural economies, based primarily on agriculture and trade, metamorphosed into an urban, industrialised and mechanised economy.

The Industrial Revolution marked a turning point in history, modifying and influencing all aspects of daily life in one form or another. Both agricultural production and nascent industries multiplied whilst production time decreased. From 1800 onwards, wealth increased and there were more rich people than ever before. For the first time in history, the standard of living of the masses and common people experienced sustained growth in quality. There is nothing remotely like this economic development at any time in the past.

Thus, began a transition that would end centuries of manual labour and the use of animal traction. They were replaced by machinery for industrial manufacturing and the transport of freight and passengers. This transition began at the end of the 18th century in the textile industry and with the extraction and use of coal. The expansion of trade was possible thanks to the development of communications through the construction of railways, canals and roads.

The transition from a fundamentally agricultural economy to an industrial economy greatly influenced the lives of the population. Rapid growth was witnessed, particularly in urban areas. The introduction of the steam-driven pump engine to support various industries was the definitive step in the success of this revolution, as its use meant a spectacular increase in production capacity and movement of goods. Later, the introduction of steamboats and railways, as well as the development in the second half of the 19th century of the electric motor and energy, represented unprecedented technological progress. As a consequence of industrial development and its emerging social scale, new groups or classes were born. The vast majority of the population fell into the working class bracket, embracing industrial labourers and poor peasants toiling in the countryside. Separately, a new economic class known as the "bourgeoisie" arose. These were the owners of the means of production and holders of most of the capital generated by economic activity.

All these changes sharpened over time. The first Industrial Revolution was followed by a period of transition (1840-1870) that would be the prelude to the second Industrial Revolution. This later revolution entailed many changes, especially in technology. With the onset of the First World War in 1914, this stage would draw to a close, but the economic and social model based on capitalism would continue to develop. Our model of happiness, upon which we are analysing in this book, is rooted in the culture and norms which emerged from the onward march of capitalism across the world.

Most of us have become accustomed to a certain lifestyle that seems easy, monotonous and even boring when compared to the challenges of everyday existence faced by our ancestors. In modern times, with a more moderate way of living, and having satisfied our basic needs for food and housing, we have the basic ingredients of what many, but not all, would describe as happiness.

Chapter 2

Parameters of happiness

Today, in the Western world, people have a generalised idea of what can make them happy. We no longer have that strong bond, as we did in prehistoric times, with the community; we are more individualistic. Consumer society has transcended all levels, even the most spiritual. When we have acquired something like a car or a house, the momentary happiness soon disappears and we want something else. We think that we have more freedom today, but it is very difficult for us to be satisfied if we are not constantly acquiring something, e.g. a house, a new partner, a type of employment or trips away. "Having" has replaced "being". When we disconnect from our spirit, doubts and confusion arise. Then, we often feel very lonely.

Now, what can we do to dispel this dissatisfaction? If we thought about what ingredients are necessary for a happy life, what would you say? There must be some signs or some indicators that guide us as to what to throw away. What factors, parameters or criteria govern a full life? It may not be so difficult to recover our true self. Next, we will analyse the main points or references that can help us to recognise a happy environment.

Examples of factors that influence our happiness to a greater or lesser extent

- Although **the weather** in our locality may affect us at a specific time, it cannot claim to be a major player in our quest for happiness.
- On the other hand, **social coexistence**, i.e. the relationship with other people, is extremely important. It is easier to be happily integrated into life in a group, association or team than it is being isolated and alone, without friends and without going out to engage with the world. In fact, the only external element, statistically proven, that differentiates happy people from those who are not so happy, is the degree to which they engage in SOCIAL NETWORKS and the extent to which they spend time with friends or family. Those who have more friends are usually happier and enjoy life more.
- Having **a satisfying relationship** with a partner that helps us grow as a person is a basic component of happiness. An interesting variant of this view is that even if the partnership is stable, if it does not make us a better person it can stagnate our growth and can even make us very unhappy.
- A full, satisfying **sexual relationship** can make us feel happy; there is no doubt. If you do not have

a partner, you do not have to worry. Sex is not everything.

- **Gratitude** and forgiveness to others are fundamental requirements to help us be at peace and feel good about ourselves.
- **Envy, bad mood and anger** are not signposts for happiness, rather, they alienate us from it.
- **Staying active** makes us happier, i.e. living for the moment so that everything we do makes us feel alive.
- **Savouring the simple things** that we see every day, such as a field of poppies, listening to the singing of birds or hearing the laughter of a child offers happiness. These sensations equate with a positive appreciation of the world.
- Knowing that one can choose **freedom** contributes to making our existence worth fighting for.
- **Always looking for pleasure** does not automatically mean that we are going to be happier. Sometimes, searching for pleasure makes us focus too much on our ego. Feeding habits which, although they may not be entirely harmful, in the end do not help us to move forward on our path towards glimpsing real happiness.
- **Money is not the basis for happiness**. Each person gives it a very different value and it is a very relative factor when it comes to influencing our happiness. In fact, many things that cost us money cannot give us happiness; you cannot buy happiness. Moreover, it has been shown that people who love money are more dissatisfied than those who do not place such a high value on it.

- Although it is difficult to be happy without having anything material at all, paradoxically, when we achieve true happiness we do not need anything, since it is enough for us to exist at peace with ourselves.

- In short, the factors that can make us more or less happy depend very much on each person, and in this case, on you. Only we are responsible for our happiness. If you have come this far in your reading, take things calmly. If you desperately seek happiness, you will not find it! If you are not happy, it does not mean that you cannot attain anything. It is about valuing our life more, and about fighting with a passion to give it a radical turn towards happiness. The search for pleasure does not have much to do with it. On the other hand, a committed life does have a lot to do with it.

We have analysed a wide list of factors or indicators that can influence the achievement of our personal happiness. However, these external conditioning factors are not essential. In fact, we can investigate something else, a state more related to our inner self and to our deepest feelings.

The influence of genes

Even though the truth and the way are within us, we cannot ignore the external, i.e. what happens around us. At this stage, we have not yet reached the maturity of being able to analyse our innermost self. It is a matter of going step by step.

Thus, if we look at the question from an objective point of view, a factor that can affect our happiness and which, in some way, we already carry at birth, is the character or temperament of our parents. We inherit, to a great extent, the state of mind of our most direct ancestors. It is estimated that 25 to 50 per cent of our ability to be happy comes from genes. From there, we add the rest. This may seem negative at first glance, especially if someone has or had parents with a tendency to see the bad side of things. If we do not change the habit of seeing the course of life events, i.e. as the popular expression says from "a half-empty bottle to one that is half-full", we run the risk of never appreciating full enjoyment of life. We might even persuade ourselves to think that there is no future.

Do not despair, since for almost everything there is always a remedy. Although the genetic, and surely also educational, subject matter weighs heavily, we still have a large margin of work to enable us to be happy. The brain is elastic; it changes with time and we can train a little every day to improve our outlook on life. Firstly, we must learn from and rectify our bad experiences and memories, and then remember and strengthen the good ones. It is a challenge worth trying. Whenever we can, we should look for or find things that fill us with optimism and positivity.

Exercise

What factors do I have for and against achieving happiness? Please write your opinion in your workbook. Thank you.

Now, before reading more, if you were asked right now what makes you happy, what would your answer be?

If your answer is one of the following categories, i.e. money, health or love, think about it before you go on. Try to be more specific; there are simple things that bring us a sense of being at peace with the world and this often elusive concept that we call "happiness". We will be examining this further during the course of this book.

Optimism and pessimism

Strangely enough, being active, doing positive things, helping others and expanding our social networks brings us happiness. Our perceptions are important when it comes to being happy. People tend to look more at the negative side of things. Sometimes, it seems to us that there are more negative or pessimistic people than the opposite. Nevertheless, the optimist is always more realistic.

Depression could be defined as an extreme state of pessimism. It is not only our ideas that depress or lift us; it is our moods and the way we allow these to shape our thoughts and feelings. One negative aspect of mood change is that we are drawn away from focusing on the beautiful, the positive and the wonderful things in life. We are driven to highlight the negative, sad and difficult sides of life to the point where we give more importance to them than the positive. We can even negatively distort events. We need to remember that we can always do something to help improve our lives.

Optimists persevere in choosing to find solutions to problems and inconveniences that arise. The feeling that they are in control of events and have the power to be proactive in solving difficulties helps them to remain on the bright side of life. Positive individuals study the pros and cons of a given situation in greater depth. Pessimists, meanwhile, concentrate on the negative view of almost anything, from bemoaning the poor weather to making themselves believe that they encounter nothing but bad luck. For example: "I am in a traffic jam. I knew I shouldn't be in this lane. It's always the same for me."

Thinking positively, we are more prepared to face and solve the situations that come our way more satisfactorily in terms of both the good and the not so good. Psychologists are convinced that the power to repair adversity is independent of age, intelligence, academic training or economic resources. Self-confidence and hope are strong shields in our fight against adversity.

We can all be happy

Regardless of culture, religion, country or habitat, we all have the power to achieve happiness. Reaching this goal can become a reality but it is not attained by chance. We cannot achieve it instantaneously within a period of 24 hours. Let us convince ourselves that we need to train ourselves to be happy. What prevents us from trying, then? Let us take a simple example. An athlete trains to run further and further. He disciplines himself daily to be faster, stronger and to build up resistance, preparing his body and his mind. With time and practice, he achieves optimal results.

Now let us sit down and reflect on whether you agree with the following concepts.

We need to condition our minds with positive things, i.e. with:

- motivation;
- a cheerful, positive attitude; and
- habits and behaviour that promote our well-being.

After a short period of time, having taken a turn in direction towards optimism, we will begin to feel better. Once this is achieved, we can feel at ease with ourselves and accept ourselves as we are. Whatever we define as happiness is then but a short step away.

Let us take an amusing example that will give us a lot to think about. Let us suppose that we go on a trip in an enormous, impressive sailing ship with the wind behind her and in full sail. Suddenly, we see an island in the distance covered in lush green vegetation. As we approach, the island seems even more beautiful and becomes increasingly larger. This is the Island of Happiness. If, when you first see the island, you take off in another direction you will, most likely, never reach this island of dreams. That is exactly what occurs with happiness. If you take the path of stress, envy, worries, unhealthy habits, anxiety, negative thoughts and depression of self-imposed suffering, where will you be heading?

The journey itself is not an entirely easy one. We will need to practise hard to think positively, to eliminate negative feelings such as envy and resentment towards other people and to stop the obsession with minor inconveniences that grow into major stumbling blocks. At the same time, we should promote and encourage healthy habits in our own lives, such as taking proper rest and caring for others. Bad practices acquired over significant periods of time are often difficult to erase from our lives, but it is important to persevere in order to promote psychological and physical well-being.

Multiple examples could be added, but these simple reflections are just a small sample of what you could or should work on. The global educational system we have today does not adequately advise students about the promotion of true happiness. We have good schools and universities where young people are educated and where they prepare to have a career or develop a trade. Although this may shape a profitable or secure future for them, little is done to help students recognise the significance of a structured approach to our innermost feelings.

Currently, scientists are studying different pathologies and mental illnesses, such as anxiety, stress, depression and psychological suffering. We have good psychologists, good psychiatrists and good doctors who are trained to help us with our mental trauma. If such suffering cannot be completely eliminated, at least it is addressed and controlled. However, none of these professionals can cure us of "unhappiness". I would say to them "has not the time come for us to be happy?" Looking at the subject from this angle, it will be less hard for us to consider happiness as a reality. You may think "is it really possible to be happy?" Or, "can unhappiness be transformed into happiness?" If this were such an easy issue, many people would already be happy. However, it is a harsh reality that the world is filled with many worried people who are denied the state of happiness that we are alluding to in this book.

This book is not meant to be a magical solution. It is not a text that, after having been read, instantly transports the reader into a happy human being, nor is the author a magician or sorcerer endowed with great powers. Yes, promoting happiness is the object of the book but it is also the logical result of our becoming more conscious of ourselves, of learning one lesson after another along the way. This journey to happiness is not a garden of roses, but despite everything, it is possible to be happy. It can be done. Think that living here and now, in this moment, is our most precious gift. We are fortunate because we exist.

Happiness can be seen as a radical idea and as a state that is difficult to attain. It is our attitude, our lifestyle and our actions which help us to be well. At this point, I have to emphasise something very important; I can be happy because I have passed an exam or a driving test, but the continuing state of happiness is found on a different level of being. This state is permanent in us and does not depend on external factors; we carry it in our hearts. We need to eliminate all negative factors from our lives whatever they may be, otherwise, their chains will trap us in the prison of unhappiness. We must not forget that we also have to resolve our internal conflicts. We can always transform the negative into the positive.

Reflect a little, now. Happy people are kind, positive, energetic and creative. They may have the same or more problems than their unhappy fellow human beings, but the big difference is their ATTITUDE to daily challenges. Paying attention to our mental attitude to life is of prime importance.

What is the meaning of life?

We will conclude this section with a question that could very well include all the factors that influence us at the time of being happy. In fact, its absence is a clear indicator that something is not working in our life. Happiness is closely related to the meaning of life or what the Japanese call "ikigai", i.e. the reason for living.

If we think about this phrase for a considerable period of time, we observe that "the meaning of life" implies a direction towards "something". This is a reason, or a motive. In society, "meaning" has traditionally been assigned to a woman's life, i.e. whether she gives birth, takes care of children or takes care of the family. A parallel motive is seen with men and their work. If a man does not have employment or if he has a job that does not satisfy him at all, sometimes his life seems to be aimless. In our civilisation, the meaning of life and social function are often confused or incorrectly identified. However, this may have little to do with the happiness we all desire. The meaning of life to which we allude is something that underpins, and is at the heart of, all our activities. In our childhood or youth, many of us see or feel our "direction", or our clear "reason for being". It seems as if, at birth, life has given it to us as a gift. As the years go by, events, whether positive or negative, or whether we are led to excessive activity or submit to a comfortable life, make us lose sight of our motive to wake up each morning feeling in harmony with ourselves and with the environment. More than 2,000 years ago, the philosopher Aristotle said in his writings that "the meaning of life is to be happy." For Aristotle, this was the ultimate purpose of existence.

The reason for living must be sought within us and must not be conditioned by external factors. It is something which seems so simple, but it is often not taken into account. As we have already pointed out, the succession of daily activities, to which we unthinkingly commit ourselves, blinds us when we think of our true reason for living. Stress or excessive comfort can exert a harmful influence on our existence because it does not allow us to be conscious of or realise what really matters to us, i.e. what it is that we need to be fulfilled.

Chapter 3

Am I happy?

Who has not asked himself at some time in his life this simple, but transcendental question? No matter how little you think about it seriously, you will see that it is not a question as easy to answer as it may seem. If the answer is an immediate "yes", well congratulations; you may not need to read this book. If, after listening to yourself a little, you discover that you have some degree of dissatisfaction, reading on may be useful to you.

Let us return to the initial question, i.e. "are we really happy with our life at the moment?" In all probability, your answer will be more like "yes, but..." or perhaps "I don't know". Some people may not even be able to pronounce the word "happy", making it impossible for them to define anything coherent. When our answers appear confused, it may be a result of the many problems that overwhelm us, stopping us from thinking about ourselves. Perhaps, the conflicting dynamics of each day have plunged us into a state of inertia and numbness. In either case, we are only minimally aware of our true state of mind.

Frequently, not everything is so white; not everything is so black. When this happens it is even more difficult to answer our own questions. However, the authentic answer will always come from our heart. Depending on our degree of sincerity and, of course, courage, we may be able to dive deep into our own being and discover our innermost self.

This apparently simple, or even childish, question is actually very necessary in this book. It is a knock on "a door". A first contact with our consciousness. It is the beginning of our journey.

Well, once we have realised that WE ARE NOT HAPPY, or that we lack something to be totally so, the time has come to act. *Happiness in the 21ˢᵗ Century* is intended to help you do this whenever you want to. Doing something to improve our state of mind involves embracing motivation and action. In this sense, this book WILL ENCOURAGE YOU and urge you to act thanks to its advice and proposals.

Once we are aware of our situation here and now, let us ACT. By taking "action" we must consider two important aspects, i.e. not to postpone what we want to do until the following day, and to concentrate on making a change for the better right now.

"Do not put off until tomorrow what you can do today."

This well-known proverb could very well illustrate the first step to begin our journey. Do not leave things until the next day. DO NOT POSTPONE anything; that would be the key. The problem is that tomorrow becomes today and the inclination to avoid action repeats itself. The tomorrow that appears in your mind never appears as the present. Many people believe they have skills for creativity. Most of the time, however, they think that they will do it "one day", but the truth is that their commitment to creating a new life, a new job or fresh relationships is put on hold indefinitely. You may ask yourselves "how does that happen?"

We often sideline ideas, e.g. "I'll do it tomorrow when I have more free time", or "when the children have left home". If we procrastinate, we may not be able to develop our creativity or trust ourselves to do it. We may have negative ideas about ourselves of which we are not even aware. Sometimes, they are hidden beneath the surface of daily activity, or we often fool ourselves with an infinite variety of excuses.

Some negative ideas might be:

- I do not have a good job;
- I do not get paid well at work;
- I do not get promoted in my job;
- I do not have good friends;
- I do not know how to speak in public;
- I do not like my physical appearance;
- I do not like my family; or
- I do not like my life in general.

Start changing right now

Now that we can see that we should not put things off, let us consider the second aspect of the issue. We must begin to

CHANGE TODAY, NOW and at this very moment. This may seem easy, but in reality, our psyche is too accustomed to function in a certain way. As we observe ourselves a little, we will realise that our reactions to outside factors follow a similar path.

Most of the time, we have faculties to develop, whether manually, artistically or intellectually. We can all be good at something once in a while. Regardless of age or situation, even if it might at first seem impossible, we can all learn, for example, to play an instrument, to fix the garden well, to write a poem, to study something interesting in our free time, to do another job or even to speak a new language.

We must stop putting up barriers which stand in the way of our progress, otherwise limitations close in on our thought processes. If we transform our way of thinking, we will see that in a relatively short period of time, things around us will change significantly. We will do things we have always wanted to do!

Instead of thinking "tomorrow I'll do this or that," I need to think "I'll do it right now, right now," and then "I'll do it, really". Once we do this for a few months and on a regular basis, we will start noticing changes. We will have more time to do more things. We will feel better, more positive and encouraged to do even more. We will feel more alive.

It is never too late for you to be the person you have always wanted to be.

At this point, you may think that if this were so easy, why are so few people doing it?

When people settle into what they might view as stability, be it economical or be it emotional, many sink into what could be referred to as a comfort zone where they let life float into and over them unquestioningly. In other words, they adapt to lifestyles and habits that have become more pleasurable, i.e. ones which require less effort. By adopting such habits, whether it be consciously or unconsciously, they reject the changes that life has in store for them. In short, they opt for a simple life, doing the same thing day after day without complicating their existence and without thinking too much about the world around them. In this state of inertia, we stop living fully, choosing instead to react negatively and letting pass the opportunities that our precious existence offers us. We are very comfortable doing what we have always done, resisting change again and again. Faced with this situation, what should we do? Begin to IMAGINE the changes we want to make in ourselves. Incredible as it may seem, if we spend a while doing just that, things will start to happen around us.

The way we see ourselves in the here and now has its origins in childhood, i.e. the way we were treated by our parents, friends, neighbours, teachers and siblings. All these experiences happened in our lives before.

Chapter 4

Transforming the way of thinking

If we stop putting things off until tomorrow and stop resisting change, we will be on the road to happiness. It is true that, despite knowing this, we do just the opposite and it is very difficult for us to put these new designs into practice. This is owing to our mistaken way of thinking, which constantly creates and feeds the NEGATIVE IDEAS that we form. Frequently, this accumulation of negative becomes a cloud that prevents us from seeing where the cause of our unhappiness or dissatisfaction lies. Thus, to recognise where our main problem really stems from becomes a very complex issue. We are then left asking ourselves where we can concentrate our efforts to obtain the best results.

So, if we "think badly", whatever that might entail, we must LEARN TO THINK WELL, or correctly. Changing the way of thinking may seem difficult, however, this book offers you a series of guidelines to achieve it. Like all training, it needs motivation, perseverance and patience, but the result, as incredible as it may seem, will be surprising. By changing your way of thinking, your whole person will be transformed for the better, and at a much deeper level than you could ever imagine.

From negative to positive

We cannot be happy if we continue with negative thoughts towards ourselves and towards the image of our life that we portray to ourselves and the rest of the world. When you believe in yourself, you will see that everything around you stimulates the creation of a positive and happy environment. We must learn to accept, love and pamper ourselves.

It is essential that our self-esteem notably improves. It must be high in order to achieve our goal of happiness. In essence, we are all much the same at birth, but over the years we have created negative thoughts about ourselves. Feeling comfortable in our own skin and in our own body, and being more sociable, creative, flexible and kind to others and to ourselves can all be indications that you are already on the road to happiness. This is where your ability to choose comes in, i.e. your freedom, because it is solely your responsibility to set to work to achieve it.

So, we must remove from our mind, or at least not promote, ideas such as:

- I cannot do this;
- I do not have time;

- I have many things to occupy me all the time;
- I am too old to change;
- I will do it later, although every day I say the same thing to myself, and in the end I never do;
- I do not have the energy to change;
- I am afraid of change;
- I will never be perfect; or
- I do not trust myself.

These ideas create distrust, insecurity and negativity in ourselves. If these thoughts continue to come to our mind, we must STOP THEM AND ATTEMPT TO THINK POSITIVELY. Thus, we can repeat positive phrases during the day, and little by little, things will start to improve.

In short, if you yearn for happiness and dream of being happy, you have to move, do things and work at it. It is important to get to work on the challenge right away. If you continue to let yourself go and settle into a comfort zone both mentally and physically, it will be difficult for you to enjoy life in its fullness. After an adjustment to our way of looking at ourselves, and at the wider world, happiness has every chance to follow. I will tell you honestly, however, that it will not appear unaided, you have to work on it. The exercises I recommend in this book will help you. You do not really have much to lose. You will always feel better than you did before, and with renewed ideas you will come to better understand your social environment, thus improving your family ties and working relationships.

I can give you a simple, practical example. If you are going to live in a large modern city, you will need to know some important places, such as the post office, the town hall or the local schools. So far as happiness is concerned, the same kind of guidance is required. We need to have a position marker or map to enable us to find the points or pillars by which we can learn to be happy.

I want to emphasise that it is not easy to achieve happiness simply by wanting to be happy or by just thinking about happiness, although these feelings could be seen as a starting point.

Now, please write in your notebooks five positive things that you will put your mind to for at least two weeks.

This does not mean that you have to abandon your efforts after two weeks. If you have time and long-term dedication you must of course continue with them. We have to find out what we are good at, whether this is hobbies, work or sport, and dig deeper.

Think of yourself as stronger than you think. You have to understand why your life is the way it is now. We are capable of controlling our inner world, but we have to work with determination to achieve it. Thanks to our motivation to want to be happy we can train ourselves to transform our mindset. Another step will be to VISUALISE images, situations and events that we would like to happen, i.e. events that we believe would make us happy. It is important at this point to be realistic and not to build unattainable castles in the air.

Having your feet on the ground is essential to advance along the path you have embarked on. Then, THINK, but within a framework of achievable goals.

Changing our way of thinking is entirely possible. It is about REPLACING NEGATIVE IDEAS WITH POSITIVE ones. This is an essential step and I can give an example. Think of a late-model sports car, elegant, beautiful and fast. You drive it, but with the handbrake on. Would you not think that there is something odd? Negative ideas could be responsible for having the brake on. Such ideas can be compared to ballast which many times, without us realising it, cancels out our aims and aspirations and prevents us from being ourselves.

The thoughts and attitude that we adopt now, our positive and negative ideas and our subsequent actions, will all have an enormous impact on the coming years of our lives, and will influence the things that happen around us, whether at work, with the family or simply with our partners and friends.

You can see for yourself how important it is to think positively, and to try to be strong inside. We can change many things about ourselves by being open-minded and by taking advantage of the good opportunities that come our way in life. We need to make the most of them.

Write in your workbook at least two pages about what your ideal life would be like, i.e. something reasonable, possible and realistic. Then, take your time and write down the steps you need to take to achieve it.

We must prevent the things that happen to us in life from becoming out of control. We may not be able to change the climate, our politicians or the driver of the bus that we take every morning, but what can and should be changed are the events that directly affect us. We cannot go thinking all our lives that we are always the victim. We must try to learn from our experiences and become emotionally balanced. Do not make excuses for not taking responsibility in your life for your own actions.

Every night we should GIVE THANKS for what we have in life, and for the good things that it gives us. They say that "to be born well is to be thankful". It is very important to be grateful for everything that comes to us in this life. Creation is always beautiful, and we are part of that beauty. To show appreciation for everything that happens to us and believing that we are the better for it is a truly positive concept.

The better you feel, both physically and psychologically, the more on track you will be in reaching your goal of happiness. Life will seem more acceptable, light-hearted and fun-filled when you understand that it is only ourselves who put the limitations on what we can or cannot achieve.

You may be one of the many who think that the world needs to be changed into a more just and peaceful place, where no one goes hungry. Fine, but why do you not make a starting point yourself? One of the finest attitudes that we can adopt is that we love the life we live, appreciate that we are surrounded by caring family, and of course, many friends.

The economic powers of the world will say that "time is money" and that we have to apply this to our lives. Whilst guided by the economic realities of living, we need to take time out for ourselves in order to do the things we have always wanted to do.

Write in your notebook the names of ten people who caused you problems in your childhood or youth. Then, write down the things they did to you that you did not like at the time. Then, write down how you felt at that moment, and what your reaction to them was.

Then, visualise these people and forgive them for their actions. It does not matter if they are no longer amongst us. You will be able to observe how by doing this simple exercise; you will feel calmer and more at peace. To do this, you cannot hold any kind of grudge or resentment in your heart.

Something important when changing and training our mind is to LEARN TO ORDER OUR IDEAS. In this way, we can organise our "positive" ideas as if they were our own home. We need to live in an orderly place so that we can be calm. The same thing happens in our office at work. We will try to keep everything clean and tidy, both inside and out.

We must respect and love ourselves. Think now of your own religion or spiritual beliefs. Any religion that condemns us or makes us feel guilty for existing is either not right or not well-interpreted or practised.

The influence of others

For the end of this chapter, we have left a point that may well affect us very much, i.e. the influence that others, especially those closest to us, exert on us.

Most of the time and unconsciously, we project an idea on something external to ourselves which is fictitious and not real. We often think that others are better people and have a fuller and happier life than we do. This practice indicates that we underestimate ourselves and that we do not appreciate each other on a face-to-face basis rooted in reality.

Our being is weakened when we lose our inner strength, and it is then that we let ourselves be affected by others, or rather, by the idea we have formed of them. We are then in danger of losing our path and of letting go of the reins of life.

We can be kind to others, listen to them, try to understand them and openly accept their advice. This does not mean that we always have to act or think like them; this would be incorrect. We may think that someone we know may have a wonderful, perfect life, but you may know few things about that person, and in reality, that person may not be entirely happy, despite appearances. The same can happen to others, in reverse. They might see you and others as high achievers or as their idols, and think that you are very happy, even though it is not true. In short, often we allow ourselves to be influenced by ideas about others that ARE NOT REAL. Since these thoughts are not true, they also have a negative influence on us and so we must eliminate them or replace them with others that <u>are</u> real or true. The truth can be found in the observation of the real world. Things should not be taken for granted. To know how to listen and to look at what surrounds us is crucial.

Once we have analysed the negative aspect that the influence of others can exert on us, let us observe the positive part. Other people are essential for us to live happily and to have a balanced existence. Surrounding ourselves with positive friendships and calm, happy and peaceful people can help us a great deal in establishing our self-esteem and finally, in the attainment of happiness. The harmony of these relationships will activate our inner power to remain physically and psychologically well. It is imperative that we do things with passion and joy. We can observe and hear the opinions that others have of us, but always with a critical spirit. If we listen more to ourselves, it will help give us the ability to discern what is true and what is not. Montaigne was a French philosopher of the 16th century; a phrase from one of his works became very famous, i.e. "one of the greatest things in the world is to know oneself."

Chapter 5

My thoughts motivate me

Once we have taken stock of our situation and whether or not we are confronting unhappiness or dissatisfaction, we have pushed the button for "all systems go". Despite the magnitude of the problem or problems, we think we have decided to "ACT NOW". Already, we are at the start of our journey to happiness as free beings, which, in essence, all of us are. We have chosen to work to achieve our goal, a state of happiness that will not only benefit ourselves but also the people around us.

Travelling this path will mean transforming our mind. We have pointed out in the previous chapter that we must keep track of our thoughts and identify negative ideas. First, we have to imagine what we want our life to be like from now on. A general vision, of knowing how we are going and where we want to go, will motivate us to continue with our work. With daily practice, we will learn to dismiss negative thoughts and feelings and substitute them for others of a positive nature. With patience, little by little, we will not only transform our way of thinking, but this change will penetrate all layers of our being. Then, it will be like moving the first piece of a domino set. By creating positive ideas out of negative ones, we will feel fresh ideas engulfing us as if they had been won by sheer tenacity. Now, a new form of thinking will be our guide and will make us flourish as increasingly positive and dynamic beings.

However, changing our mindset may seem easy, but it is not; we must prepare the ground for it and alter some possibly long-established habits. Above all, it is important to eliminate the harmful ones and take up ones which we consider to be for our future physical and psychological well-being.

What do I think?

Most people are not aware of the degree to which negative thoughts can impact on their lives throughout the day. This influences everything that happens to us, generating a way of living that could be very harmful to us. This negativity can appear spontaneously. At other times, we are aware that such feelings of low esteem may be influenced by past situations which we have never been able to come to terms with.

We need to be more aware of what we think and try to replace all negative thoughts with positive ones. If we notice that some of our thoughts are not entirely positive, we simply have to reject them as being of very secondary importance, and then we will need to address our journey to happiness once more.

You may think that this is easier said than done, but if you get used to practising a little every day, you will succeed. In fact, just by devoting some time to daily practice, you will notice how much positive benefit you have achieved after just a few weeks.

If you think that everything in itself is too complicated, maybe it is. However, read and write down your answers. Is it true that everything is complicated or do I make it complicated? Stop for a moment, rethink and analyse the thoughts that are running through your mind at that very moment. Do you control those thoughts or do they control <u>you</u>? Write the answer in your notebook.

Is it true that you want to change your life? Or, are they just vague ideas, a permanent dream and illusion that we always repeat to ourselves so that the pathway to change becomes a journey we never begin. We always make excuses not to start, e.g. "today, I don't have time", "tomorrow I can't" and "the day after tomorrow, I have to go to the cinema". Think and write about how you are going to change your life from now on.

If you become aware that your thoughts are negative right now, stop them immediately and try to repeat positive ones to yourself if you are alone, or to friends if you are with them.

Exercise 1

Find a quiet place with no noise, no music and no interruptions. Turn off your mobile phone.

Sit comfortably, close your eyes and take five deep breaths. Relax for a few minutes and concentrate on your breathing. Do not concentrate on anything in particular, just relax.

Once calm, we will visualise in our mind the changes that we want to make in our life to be happier. This exercise could last half an hour. Later, you can write down what you have visualised. If you can do this exercise a couple of times a week, it will bring you closer and closer to your goal.

Exercise 2

For a week, at the end of the day, write down the seven most positive thoughts that come to mind. Do the same with the seven most negative thoughts you have on a daily basis, preferably before going to bed.

After a week you will be able to compare them, and you will see how most, if not all of them were unnecessary and inappropriate.

You may think that you do not have much time to do this exercise, but if you do, you will come to realise how many negative thoughts we have each day. If we analyse this in a rational way, we will be able to appreciate how harmful each instance can be.

Exercise 3

First, we will concentrate and try to be calm and relaxed to become aware of our inner self.

Find a quiet room, without noise of any kind, but where it is warm. At the beginning of the exercise, sit in a comfortable chair with a straight back. After a few sessions, you can lie down to do the following exercises.

Imagine a forest with lots of trees, plants and shrubs. The sun shyly pierces through the clearing of the tree-tops. Now, you begin to walk along a path, and in the distance you see what looks like a small wooden hut. In front of it, there are two big green firs. Smoke comes out of the chimney.

You decide to enter the little hut. You knock on the door and it opens itself. Once inside, you can see a table with four chairs in the middle of the room and a painting featuring a large sailing boat hanging behind the table. To the left of the table is a black bed. You lie down on it; it is soft and comfortable. You relax and then come face-to-face with your inner self. In this way, your character and personality will be reinforced, giving you more security. You relax for ten minutes or so.

Now, go back to visualisation. Then, you get up from the bed, leave the cabin and go back the same way to where you started from. Then, you become aware that you are sitting in the chair. Open your eyes and take three deep breaths, breathing in through your nose and out through your mouth. Get up slowly. Feel how relaxed and calm you are now.

This exercise, practised a few times a week, will reinforce your mental strength.

Good habits

The road to happiness may seem long and even hard but like every thought, it is relative. If I want to go hiking in the mountains, for example, I can always take a shortcut to get to the top. You just have to know how to look and choose the right path. Something similar happens with the road to happiness. The shortcut to making the path easier lies in having GOOD, HEALTHY HABITS. This does not mean that they are the ones that we like the most.

Some things that we should value in our habits are:

- Serenity;
- Daily exercise;
- Personal cleanliness;
- Thinking positively;
- The art of living correctly, i.e. the way in which we live and think today determines, to a great extent, our state of mind;
- It is essential to be calm. Worries, and the stress that is often part of our lives, cause our body to have high levels of harmful stress hormones. We need more time to rest and relax; and
- Work a little with this book daily.

If you follow these guidelines, you will be surprised at how your life will improve after just a few months. You may think "what a long time!" Well, let us be frank and honest with ourselves. You could achieve it sooner, but you would have to have more free time. Think that many people are never happy in their lives. So, after all, about five or six months is not a lot of time to ask.

Try to reduce the stress in your life on a daily basis and control the moods you have every day. Change your approach to life; there is always something to see from a positive angle. The quality of our lives depends largely on our physical and mental health. Stress is associated with the way we live. It manifests itself in the everyday aspects of our lives, i.e. at work, with the family or in our social environment. Stress has a very negative impact; it is as if we were burdened with large chains. This example is exaggerated, but intentionally so, in order that we become more aware of the reality of our situation.

Many people think that they can always go to the doctor when they have too much stress. This, dear reader, is not the solution either. The real objective is to prepare oneself mentally and physically to be better and to achieve a happier and more fulfilling life.

Practical measures that we can gradually introduce into our lives include:

- Laugh more often and rarely get angry;
- At first try to change your status quo in a light and simple way;
- People often lead very sedentary lives although our body is capable of a lot of daily activity, and so do more sport, even if moderately so; and
- Most people do not recognise, or want to recognise, the degree to which each of us can go to achieve a healthier life.

Chapter 6

A fundamental pillar: health

Happiness is in some way directly related to health. This does not mean that a healthy person is necessarily happy, nor does it mean that a person who is ill cannot be happy. However, there is a strong body of evidence that the body and mind are somehow linked. When something goes wrong in one part, if the situation persists, it is very probable that it will have consequences in the other. One example could be a person who is very stressed by work over a period of months and who eventually develops a stomach or skin condition. Nowadays, many health centres have a psychosomatic unit as an addition in order to address just such issues. Psychosomatic medicine is an interdisciplinary medical field exploring the relationships amongst social, psychological and behavioural factors on bodily processes and quality of life. The body, the mind and, if you like, the spirit or the soul are closely linked. Today, many alternative therapies of a holistic nature focus on healing the person, concentrating initially on his or her psychology.

Health is a state of well-being or equilibrium that can be seen at a subjective level, where a human being assumes the general state in which he finds himself to be acceptable, or at an objective level, i.e. the absence of disease or harmful factors. The term "health" stands in contrast to that of "disease", and is today the focus of medicine and the health science industries. Health is conceived as a framework in which a person can enjoy physical and psychological harmony in dynamic interaction with the environment in which he or she lives. Health is primarily a measure of each person's ability to be well. It is the dynamic balance of risk factors between the environment and us.

However, the concept of health or good health is subjective. Some people have become accustomed to living with a state of chronic ill health as if it were normal. This state of being can be influenced, amongst other reasons, by social or family environments, by personal experiences that make it difficult for people to recognise what good health could in fact mean for them, and sometimes by inappropriate support from professionals.

Now answer these simple questions:

- What do you mean by good health?
- Are you in good health?
- What can you do to improve it?
- What steps will you take to do this?

After proper consideration, write the answers in your notebook. Do not think that you do not need to write down the answers, even if you believe that you know them all and think that you are wasting valuable time. Otherwise, it will be extremely difficult for you to make the changes necessary to be happy.

Most of us, more or less, have some small idea of what these questions mean, but we rarely do anything to secure a state of good health. Becoming aware of this failure can help us to motivate ourselves more, and to start, as of today, to improve our mental and physical well-being.

Factors that can accompany poor health

Just as happiness has its parameters or indicators, such as positive social relationships, having a partner with whom one gets along well and staying active, amongst others, unhappiness also has its own markers and is often closely associated with poor mental or emotional health. In this sense, anxiety, stress and depression are common factors. Although they have different definitions, anxiety, stress and depression can be part of a set of symptoms resulting from a lifestyle imbalance. Many physical illnesses can be triggered through emotional chaos.

Now, let us pause for a moment to reflect; how are you today?

Write down your answer in your notebook, and try to reason why you feel this way. Reflect a few minutes before writing.

Try to be as honest as you can. These writings are only for you, so that you can see any improvements in your state of being as well as any benefits achieved from the exercise of this analysis.

Stress and anxiety

This initial concept comes from the English term "stress"; dictionary synonyms include "emphasis" and "pressure". It is associated with the state that occurs from events that generate anxiety or anguish. When a person is bombarded with too much information and his or her brain cannot assimilate everything, it is then that he or she may possibly begin to show signs of anxiety and depressive behaviour. It should be clarified at this point that anxiety is something other than stress, although the two may seem synonymous. Anxiety can be caused in two ways. Firstly, when there is a concrete alert that warns a person of a threat to life and limb, in response, the person generates a state of anxiety aimed at self-preservation. A simple example is on meeting a lion, a person flees for his life so as not to be attacked. The second is an unreasoned anxiety, which is not provoked by an external stimulus but generated by certain fears or phobias. This pathological anxiety can rise to the surface even when the external factor that may have triggered it has already disappeared. Stress and anxiety, as has been said, can appear to have the same root, but they do not.

The factors that cause stress are called stressors and are stimuli that reach our brain and destabilise the normal balance of the body, otherwise known, in formal terms, as the body's "homeostasis". This is the name given to the set of self-regulating phenomena that lead to the maintenance of constancy in the properties and composition of an organism's internal environment. The effects of stress change the normal functions of physiology and the way of storing all kinds of information in our brain.

Separate from the states of anxiety and depression, some symptoms related to stress can be problems of concentration, not resting well, difficulty in sleeping, social and family isolation, excessive and rapid loss of hair, permanent low mood and always seeing life from a negative perspective.

At this point, we have to mention something important. All people suffer from stress, some more than others. The medical world suggests that our personalities and attitude to life shape the level of stress to which we are subject. It is also noteworthy to remember that there is a body of evidence to indicate that optimistic people with a high self-esteem usually do <u>not</u> suffer from high stress levels.

Some tips to avoid unwanted stress can include regular exercise, daily walks, swimming and practising sport in general. It is highly recommended that people adopt activities that promote a healthy lifestyle and enjoy hobbies that bring satisfaction. It is also important that we eat slowly and do not try to do too many things at the same time. Relaxation exercises can also bring great reward, such as yoga, in its most westernised version, or following the teachings of a master. Something that can be important is to be able to enjoy meaningful, healthy friendships with people who could join you on excursions into the mountains or the countryside.

Periodically, all of us experience something that makes us feel uncomfortable. We need to show fortitude in the face of life's drawbacks. People suffering from depression lose motivation. When this depression lasts for years, it can generate both psychological and physical illnesses. Some people may suffer for years from low mood, anxiety or sleeping difficulties, yet fail to recognise the link between their symptoms and their root causes. They only know that they are feeling "unwell", resulting in their negative frame of mind spreading and seeping into relationships with family and friends.

If you think that you have some of the symptoms of depression, melancholy, anxiety, stress or similar, it is important to be aware of them and to take action against the threat that they pose to your mental and physical well-being. If necessary, seek help from a professional, a friend or even from a book like this. If a person really wants to advance their personal development and to set out on the road to happiness, a pivotal change in their approach to life is required to root out this downward spiral of negative thinking. This will help to promote a far greater sense of well-being and enjoyment of life.

Remember that loneliness and isolation from society and family are not desirable in any sense. On the contrary, we should go out, meet people, relate to others, be interested in someone, volunteer in a community or be part of a team or association. It is precisely because of this isolation that it can take some people a long time to recognise their depressive state.

We have to discover for ourselves the cause or causes of our negative frame of mind and try to reason them out in a positive way. Think first of the present, leaving the past behind. We have all made mistakes or made inappropriate decisions in the past. However, this cannot prevent us from being well now or from being happy in the future.

We should not overlook or underestimate our stress because if the situation persists, in addition to making us feel unhappy or dissatisfied, it can deepen into worsening conditions such as depression.

Another factor to keep in mind is that sometimes we are at such an emotionally low ebb that our body does not respond to medication. These stressed or depressive states sometimes manifest themselves as a prolonged period of accentuated sadness or melancholy which can also result in poor sleep patterns.

These symptoms may come because of deep-seated unhappiness. Apathy and inertia are frequent side effects. Some warning signals are:

- personal isolation;
- frequent headaches;
- loss of interest in life's pleasures, e.g. hobbies, pets or sports;
- tightening of neck and shoulder muscles;
- not being able to remember some things that we should know well;
- low mood on a daily basis; and
- never being able to feel a sense of calm.

Stress is an inseparable friend of modern life. It is curious to observe that for some people it is completely normal. However, it is important that they recognise their own limits so as to maintain a healthy lifestyle balance. On the other hand, other people, who seem to have little stress, are prone to emotional slumps. Many human beings share similar problems. Some examples are:

- strict parents;
- sad and lonely adolescence;
- financial problems;
- difficulties at work;
- death of a family member;
- problems with children or partners; and
- isolation, i.e. being without a partner or not having friends.

We do not have to carry these problems with us all the time. Mental strength is important in solving them little by little, and one by one. Incidents from the past need to be seen as one more addition to a wealth of experience.

If something more serious has happened to us, such as the loss of a family member, we have to eventually accept it as the cycle of life. All living beings are born, live in the space that is given to them and then leave one day. In cases of accident or illness, the situation for nearest and dearest becomes more dramatic. It is important, where appropriate, to offer support to those suffering potential loss of a loved one. They will need cushioning from the rest of the world during a time of grief and during their struggle to accept that life must go on. Friends and family need to provide a lifeline.

Managing our stress

Sometimes we notice that we cannot concentrate. People talk to us but it is hard for us to react. It is as if we are in the present but "not there" at the same time. Perhaps we are worried or anxious about something, and our subconscious becomes "blocked".

We need to address mental pain and emotional suffering. It is important to strike a balance before you reach your goal and channel away anger or sadness. Easier said than done, you say. Well, you are right, but see it in this perspective. Instead of saying, "this is almost impossible", put a positive spin on it, and say, "this is less easy; this needs a little more effort".

After a few weeks of thinking with a new approach to life, you will notice that you are no longer irritated or angry about things that once bothered you. You will also notice that, in many cases, you yourself were the root cause of much of your worry and impatience.

Yes, this little discovery may induce a little frustration, but think that your goal is almost there and that your happiness is the most important thing. For external changes to occur in our life, we must first have made some internal changes. We have to be ourselves and to be more analytical, positive and realistic.

Some tricks to be able to change rapidly for the better include:

- remove negative thoughts;
- think positive every day;

- love each other and accept each other;
- believe in ourselves, as we have to be in charge of our own minds;
- do not let the things that happened to us in the past condition our future as the past is past and we cannot change it;
- the present is now and "yes" we can change it; and
- we have to visualise ourselves achieving our goals in a life of happiness and love.

It all depends on you. Are you prepared and sufficiently motivated to begin the journey?

Depression

The term "depression" was derived from the Latin verb *deprimere*, "to press down". From the 14th century, "to depress" meant to subjugate or to bring down in spirits.

It is an emotional disorder that makes the person feel sad and unhappy, experiencing an inner malaise and hindering interaction with the environment. Symptoms include the desire to cry, sadness for no apparent reason, seeing things that happen to us as being always or almost always negative, and loss of appetite.

For medicine and psychology, depression manifests itself through a series of symptoms that engender mood swings, irritability, lack of enthusiasm and a sense of permanent anguish that transcends what is considered normal. In the development of depression, it is common for a combination of a high level of stress and the persistence of some negative emotions to occur. Misuse of drugs can trigger the onset of a depressive disorder.

This mood disorder would be characterised by feelings of deep pain, anger, frustration and loneliness that would eat into the quality of a normal life, possibly for a very long time.

Symptoms of this disease or condition include:

- a highly irritable mood;
- discouragement from carrying out usual activities;
- insomnia or difficulty sleeping;
- sudden increase or decrease in appetite;
- sensations of utter loneliness and helplessness; and
- suicidal thoughts.

It is important to point out that one of the most harmful symptoms of depression is the decrease in feelings of self-esteem, which triggers other complications and problems in social interaction.

In children, school attendance and performance can be significantly affected. Feelings of isolation can manifest themselves in behavioural problems.

Some types of depression are listed below.

- Post-partum depression. After giving birth some women fall into a deep well of bitterness and sadness. The most harmful characteristic of this type of depression is that the mother often feels a certain aversion for her child. For this reason, such women must receive psychological support.

- Premenstrual or dysphoric disorder. Whilst euphoria is used to describe a state of extreme happiness, ***dysphoria*** is the opposite, i.e. it is a profound sense of unease or dissatisfaction. Symptoms appear a week before the period and usually disappear when the days of the period are over.

- Bipolar disorder. Although it is not strictly considered to be a depressive disorder, it has phases which are depressive and which, without treatment, can become a serious mental illness. Its causes are believed to be genetic, i.e. passed down from parent to child, or traumatic childhood experiences that have been mischannelled. Sometimes it is enough to present with a small depressive symptom for a stressful situation to cause depression, i.e. as we would say in English, "the straw that broke the camel's back".

- We can also attribute causes such as drugs or alcohol, and in general, situations of great permanent stress to this disorder.

- Depression can be caused by cases of abuse, harassment or injustice.

- Depression may be triggered by the death of a relative, friend, partner, or in general, of someone very close.

The most serious consequences of depression can range from social isolation to the impossibility of fulfilling work tasks, even extending, in its extreme form, to thoughts of suicide. People often deny their problem or do not accept help. Nowadays, depression can be treated in many different ways, but a positive attitude on the part of the patient must always be nurtured for the successful application of any therapy.

Tips to avoid depression include:

- sleeping well for about seven or eight hours each night;
- avoiding the consumption of drugs and alcohol;
- avoiding the consumption of energy drinks;
- engaging in routine, moderate exercise; and
- keeping suicidal or extremely negative thoughts at bay.

Loneliness

Stress, anxiety or even depression are often accompanied by loneliness, which, in its most negative sense means to feel alone, regardless of whether or not we are physically alone.

In a general sense, we can say that loneliness is a lack of companionship. It is closely related to the loss of relationships, especially those of people significant to someone's life and with whom they may have interacted regularly. It tends to be linked to states of sadness, lack of love and negativity, regardless of the benefits that an occasional period of solitude can bring. Such solitude can be a voluntary spell of isolation, e.g. when the person needs to be alone, or involuntary, e.g. when the subject is alone owing to the different circumstances that life can bring. It implies the lack of contact with other people. This is a subjective feeling, as there are different degrees or nuances of loneliness that can be experienced at varying levels according to what an individual's perception of being "alone" means for them.

In principle, absolute solitude does not exist. There is always someone with whom one maintains a certain closeness, whether physical or emotional. Indeed, being alone for a certain length of time is valued by many people, and even considered as essential to rest and concentration.

However, being alone as a result of unsolicited loneliness over extended periods of time can be seen as something that causes pain and dissatisfaction. As a result, people tend to make contact via pre-arranged meetings, such as walks or outings, with others whom they might not even know or who they have not met before, but who are similarly seeking companionship.

For many people, particularly, but not always those who are younger, social engagement can be merely a platform for ego without any real concern for the feelings of others in a group. There is no sense of social responsibility. Hence, some people can still feel lonely and isolated despite the fact that they are physically surrounded by others.

On a daily basis, most relationships do not demand commitment. Television, internet, chats, forums and widespread messaging systems such as *WhatsApp* and *Facebook* are ways of being in contact without being obliged to form a committed relationship. We can free ourselves from a relationship just by turning off the screen. It can help us to have global contact on a technical level, but it cannot be defined as true companionship.

Today, our society wants to sell us loneliness on an epidemic scale. It seems that we all have to be flexible, effective, productive, fast and on time for everything. The bombardment by media, 24 hours a day and 365 days a year, connects us at all times with the rest of the world, encouraging us to adapt rapidly to numerous technological changes. It is as if we are always forced to be up to the task. This gives us the sensation of being in really close contact with others when, in reality, it is not so. At the same time, it creates a sense of obligation to the outside technical world which we can neither see nor feel. In fact, it can make us feel lonely and generate stress. In short, we can say that "disappearing" or opting out of contact is a great contemporary temptation.

We could identify three main types of solitude, of being alone or loneliness; the latter is different from the first.

(A) A person does not have an intimate friendship, or does not have a rewarding relationship with someone who satisfies them and gives them security

In today's modern life, the custom of having a partner is fully recognised. It is almost a social and cultural pressure. Few people stop to think whether or not it is now convenient or desirable to be with a partner. Perhaps we hope that the ideal person will come into our lives without the need to go out and look for them. For some, this loneliness or "aloneness" is so hard that they hold on to the first person who they are introduced to. Sometimes this does not end well, and can give rise to more problems than the loneliness itself. We have to be aware of reality, no matter how hard and raw it may be. Whether we do or do not want to live as a couple, we have to know exactly who we want, whether it be "for life" or as a temporary commitment and with or without permanent obligations.

Having established what it is we really want, we can then set out on the road to meet another who thinks as we do. If we do not do so, it will be more difficult for us to find a partner. For some people, sentimental loneliness is harder, not because they do not have intimate relationships but in order to be emotionally well, to find themselves and to grow as individuals. Most people need someone to support them, to listen to them, to spoil them and to make them feel that they are alive and that they are important. Some may enjoy an intimate relationship yet still feel emotionally alone, unable to recognise their true selves or grow as people. On the other hand, for others this is all very well in theory, but to put it into practice is almost impossible. Many find it difficult to share with their partner out of their "comfort zone." After all has been said and done, there are those who prefer to remain alone. They find it easier to follow their own individual lifestyle.

(B) Social loneliness

Loneliness could arise if we never engage in any social act. This relates directly to the ability a person has or does not have to interact with others and to express feeling. When our enthusiasm for getting to know and engaging with other people diminishes, a sense of "aloneness" embeds itself as a dominant feature of everyday existence. It usually manifests itself when we become more and more isolated and decide to stay most of the time in our "comfort zone".

When we barely communicate with family, co-workers or neighbours, loneliness becomes a regular companion. A person becomes reluctant to trust others for fear of rejection or becoming hurt. We build a wall around us, shut ourselves away in our small cell and we live the emptiness that we ourselves create. We might justify our approach with self-imposed dogmas such as "they don't understand me", "people just want to hurt me", "the only thing they are interested in is to get something out of me", or "every time you trust someone, you get a stab in the back".

If being alone, as opposed to loneliness, is what is wanted, then there can be no objection. Such a situation, however, flirts with danger; human beings are social by nature and instinctively build a network of friends with whom to share hobbies and desires. This foundation of interaction between human beings is seen as a bedrock of society and a key to what many would see as a happier life. The social structures and long-established habits of our civilisation can sometimes frustrate an effort to make and keep friends, but it is worth throwing our all into promoting and protecting this path to happiness.

Even though some become accustomed to living alone, the loneliness that accompanies this choice can create a framework for deep-seated unhappiness. This can then take the apparent form of strength, self-sufficiency, aggression or shyness, all with the aim of hiding insecurity and the fear that we will not be loved or respected.

There are also other forms of unwanted loneliness, such as that experienced by older people, by housewives working on their own during the day without external contact, by those who show an unconventional sexual orientation, those who suffer certain diseases, physical or psychological disabilities or who may be physically disadvantaged in some way.

It is important that we know how to fully differentiate between these cases:

- being alone and feeling alone;
- feeling alone when we are surrounded by people; and
- being alone and yet not feeling loneliness.

Freely express the way in which you feel loneliness. Here are some questions:

- Do you feel alone in your life?
- Have you felt lonely before?

You can answer the questions and give background details in your workbook. Now write down what you did and are doing about combatting loneliness.

When our ability to relate to others is poor, we are more likely to find ourselves alone because we are less enthusiastic about the relationships that we have and we feel less empathy with others around us. In general, those who, for whatever reason, have alienated themselves from societal integration are convinced that they are neither the kind of people who others would like to meet, nor worthy of being appreciated. They reject any kind of potential friendship in order to protect themselves against future rejection.

(C) Loss of a loved one

Whether it is through separation of a couple, the death of a loved one or another cause, when someone whom we have loved or who has played a key role in our lives disappears, we are invaded by a particular feeling of loneliness, of hopelessness and of deep-seated emptiness that plunges us into dark despair.

We are forced to confront the painful truth of being cut off from someone we have loved and who loved us, and the fear that that someone may be irreplaceable. We find ourselves lost and without a compass to help us navigate through life.

We are social beings who need others for daily interrelationships, not only to meet our needs for affection and personal development, but also to strengthen and to revalidate our self-esteem.

The damage we suffer through the loss of a loved one should not be irreparable. That gaping hole, or rather its silhouette, will remain there. However, we can move forward, albeit slowly, based on the confidence that we have in ourselves to establish new relationships that cover, at least partially, that deficit of love. We must try not to turn the loss of a loved one into a reason to cut ourselves off from the rest of the world.

This loneliness is painful, but it can become positive if we interpret it as an opportunity to learn to live through the pain without cutting ourselves off from the world and to generate resources and abilities in order to continue moving forward through life.

It is important that we recognise and respect our feelings of emotional pain, knowing that they are an inherent part of life and learning not to fear them and not to stay away from suffering them as if they were a weakness or disability. Those who know how to put their suffering into perspective are better prepared to enjoy the fullness of life in the days ahead. Solitude would be a natural and transitory state, nothing more. We must seek to make loneliness a temporary state of affairs, recognising it for what it is and not being traumatised by it. We can use it as a moment of reflection, to get to know ourselves in depth and to discover our own true identity. We need solitude to confront our own fears and to take a good long look at ourselves in the mirror of life.

There is a time to communicate with others and a time when we need to be alone in order to establish contact with the deepest part of ourselves. We have to "speak" with our fears; we cannot ignore them or let them get in the way of our happiness. It is convenient that, at times, we opt for solitude. In short, let us balance the moments in which we express ourselves and engage with others against those times that we need to think alone.

(D) Voluntary solitude

It is when we are surrounded by friends, family or co-workers, that we can decide in a totally voluntary way to isolate ourselves in order to find inner peace and calm after a time of stress, or to be able to order our thoughts and ideas. At first, as long as it is temporary, this type of solitude does not impact negatively on our lives. If it threatens to be long-term, then we will need to address the issue. However, as part of this analysis, we exclude people who freely decide to adopt a spiritual lifestyle, which may require retreat and isolation for completeness.

Some steps to overcome unwanted solitude

Write in your notebook:

Am I lonely? If the answer is "yes", continue and write:

Why do I feel lonely? Depending on your answer, find out what kind of loneliness you suffer from and the circumstances that surround it.

From this simple practice, let us try to get to know each other better. Let us put aside the fear of looking inside ourselves and face the need to know what we are really like, i.e. our dreams and ambitions, limitations and fears, who we want to be, how we are seen by others and how we look at ourselves.

Having dispensed with our shyness, let us then take the initiative to explore new relationships. Let us establish who we are interested in getting to know and develop a strategy for getting in touch with such people. There is nothing to lose. Fear of rejection acts as a deterrent to forging new friendships or loving relationships. The objective is important; let us not be squeamish.

Do not feel victimised

The world is sometimes cruel, vulgar and materialistic, okay, but surely there are other people who may be wanting to meet someone like us. To confine ourselves to ourselves is to acknowledge defeat. Most people are harmed by loneliness and so it makes us feel better to have someone to talk to, to be intimate with and to love. We are not as peculiar as we might sometimes think. Just talk in-depth with and trust another person to prove it. We can "reach" more people than we think we can, and many people outside immediate family members and those who we meet in our daily lives can be attractive to us.

Ensure you are psychologically well

Our thoughts affect our consciousness. It is important to control what goes into it and what our minds exclude from it. This determines the content and quality of our lives, making us healthier and happier. It is the ability to know how to make changes in our life that is the key to increasing our sense of enjoyment.

Looking at the social philosophy of 40 years ago, it was fashionable to explore behaviour triggered by a particular stimulus and then to analyse the response. There was also much credence given to the style of psychoanalysis proposed by the Austrian neurologist, Sigmund Freud. Both were very influential, and at the time, did not leave room for alternative investigation. Today, as part of 21st century progress, the new developments in psychology explore more modern and practical concepts where we are free to use the ability to choose.

Our emotional state affects us more than we think

People with problems at work can frequently demonstrate increased inflammatory responses, raised biochemical markers and sometimes the development of heart conditions.

Social or community activities

There are many unhappy people when the weekend comes around. It is important to make an effort to engage more with the community at large and to be active. One or two hours a week of volunteering is enough to change many people's levels of self-esteem.

In short, in order to be happy we have to put something more into our lives and something back into the society in which we live. We have to develop certain skills. There has to be an internal preparation, an effort and an investment that helps us to use our innate qualities. It is the dedication of a will to be happy and not just the desire to be happy that will enable us to turn the corner. It is not just something that happens of its own accord.

Am I really happy? We never, or hardly ever, ask ourselves this question. We have to extract the most out of ourselves and take a hard look at almost everything we do in life's different activities. It is important to bring out our strengths and focus on what we have to do and to learn from them every day. We have to take into account the choices that we have and control our anxiety when we explore them to the full. We need to think and speak positively of the world around us and not shy away from experiencing heightened emotions, one of the most rewarding being sheer joy.

It is curious to look at how human psychology has developed over thousands of years. It seems that at some stages in human history, it has even been frowned upon to be optimistic and to see positive things in life. Such an attitude has been linked in the past with naivety or even ignorance. Spain is one of the few countries in the world that had a constitution established in 1812, familiarly known as the "Pepa", which established the right of citizens to be happy. However, this is not the general rule. The philosophy of the Western world has always been "anti-emotional" and has given prominence to the rational and the logical. It has always been believed that emotions have little place in the life of someone intelligent.

It is society in its cultural contexts that gives meaning to emotions. Each one of us goes in search of this feeling of happiness, but at the same time, it is the society and the culture in which we live that, to a large extent, regulate our way of thinking.

Chapter 7

The importance of being fit

Being in good physical shape can go a long way towards contributing to our happiness. You may wonder what relation it can bring to bear on happiness. I will give you a simple but straightforward example. Imagine that you have to make a long journey by car over several days. The first thing you will do is check the car and perform a general overhaul of your vehicle. It is the same case with people. In order to be well and to be happy, it is essential to check these features, grease them and fix what is necessary, or in other words, "get into shape". The advantage of being physically well will reinforce our emotional state. As we have already pointed out, body and mind always go hand in hand. All sporting activities, properly practised, can bring balance and health to our lives. Traditionally, doctors have prescribed sport or moderate regular activity to their patients to promote psychological and physical harmony. It is crucial for us to enjoy a healthy lifestyle, e.g. a walk in the countryside, a few lengths of the pool or a bike ride. All these activities, practised with care and moderation, can enhance the quality of our lives and help us to feel well. In addition to an already-existing list of activities, I will discuss some others that can also help us to stay in good shape.

Spa centre

Although some may cast doubt on this school of thought, spa centres can form an integral part of our "keep fit" regime. A spa is a place which is usually, in the Western world at least, located in leisure centres and hotels where people from all walks of life come to relax in bathing facilities, jacuzzis and swimming pools. Spas are also called hydrotherapy centres as water is the key player in their activities, "hydro" being the Greek for water, and are closely associated with the recovery and maintenance of health. One of the origins of the word "spa" suggests that it originates in a Belgian town of the same name, which was very famous in Roman times for its healing thermal baths. Nowadays, these centres combine leisure and health activities excluding, of course, so-called medicinal waters, which in ancient times were the source around which spas developed. These centres are also ideal for the nurturing and maintenance of social relations.

The advantages of spa hydrotherapy for our health include the following:

- it activates the immune system;
- it promotes smooth functioning of the metabolism and guards against hypertension;
- it encourages muscular relaxation, relieving back, rheumatic and musculoskeletal pains;

- it also improves digestive and urinary problems;
- the spa is recommended to treat nervous diseases and conditions associated with the respiratory system;
- it relaxes the muscles and opens the pores of the skin, thus helping to eliminate toxins;
- spa treatment is recommended for tiredness and nervous tension;
- people suffering from stomach ulcers are said to have symptoms improved through spa treatment;
- it assists in recovery from bone fractures and muscle injuries; and
- spa sessions transport a person away from the outside world, relinquishing stress, focusing on both harmony and relaxation of body and mind, relieving physical discomfort.

In short, the spa encourages us to feel relaxed and rejuvenated.

Pilates

The Pilates method is a system of physical and mental training created in the early twentieth century by Joseph Hubertus Pilates (1883-1967). He based its principles on his knowledge of different specialities, such as gymnastics, traumatology and yoga. The discipline combines dynamism and muscle strength with mental control, breathing and relaxation. Its main objective is to develop internal muscles to maintain body balance and to give stability and firmness to the spine. Hence, Pilates is widely used as a therapy in rehabilitation and to prevent and cure back pain. It is practised all over the world. It owes its increasing popularity to the fact that it has been taken up by popular figures from the world of music, film, dance and sport. Pilates is based on the execution of exercises that help improve muscle tone through a series of flowing movements. The key lies in the use of the brain to control the body, promoting balance. There are two main ways of practising Pilates, i.e. to do it directly on the floor using a mat, or to engage with specially designed machines.

It is important to know that Pilates is based on six specific principles. These are:

- **concentration**, which is necessary to be able to connect the mind and body;
- **precision,** essential to perform all the movements;
- **respiratory control**, which is the basis of this discipline;
- **physical control,** which is basic to avoid uncoordinated or sudden movements that could cause physical damage;
- **fluidity of movement**, essential for the exercises to be carried out in the way that is most beneficial for the maintenance of good physical health, and also important to ensure that the movements are carried out at the correct speed; and
- **centralisation**, which establishes that the central core of the body is rooted in our abdominal muscles.

The movements designed using the Pilates method must be carried out in a conscious fashion so that they can be coordinated with breathing. Through this control of the body and mind, a Pilates devotee is able to discover both external and internal capacity. When this discipline is practised in the right way, the devotee can improve coordination, flexibility and musculature. The key to success lies in the technical precision of the movements. This has more relevance than the number of hours devoted to exercise or to the number of times that each exercise is repeated.

In addition to all of the above, we cannot overlook other important advantages of Pilates, such as how it improves a person's balance and agility. No less interesting is the fact that it helps to correct poor posture that can degenerate into back pain. It eliminates back pain; it eliminates any kind of muscular tension. Beyond the muscular and the strictly physical, the defenders of Pilates give assurances that it also helps to reduce stress and to improve the self-esteem of those who practise it. It should not be forgotten that, although anyone can carry out the practice of this discipline, it is especially recommended for people who have suffered an injury and are in the full recovery phase, and more generally for those who suffer from various back problems. Pilates can also appeal to pregnant women as it eases symptoms and stress which is triggered by knowledge of the great responsibility that is about to come into their lives. It can be recommended as a great alternative to prepare the body for the moment of childbirth, improving flexibility and strengthening the pelvic floor.

Tai_Chi

This discipline is known in the People's Republic of China as "t'ai-chi-ch'uan". In addition to being a very popular sporting activity, it is one of the martial arts practised the most on a worldwide scale. Today, several million people practise it. Depending on each individual, certain aspects of this art can be practised and developed more than others. The vast majority of people follow these techniques mainly for health reasons. Tai_Chi is also practised as a relaxation exercise or for meditation. It has spread as a competitive sport, especially in China, and particularly, amongst the younger generation. Unlike other combat sports, in Tai_ Chi there is no standardised grading system, and not all schools establish a belt hierarchy, such as the coloured one used in karate or judo. There is also no official clothing for practitioners, although it is usual to wear thin, flat-soled shoes, as well as light and comfortable clothing. Only a small proportion of Tai_Chi disciples develop it as a martial art for self-defence or as a lifestyle. In its origins, dating back over a thousand years, it is closely linked to the Taoist religion and its associated wisdom of life.

In the different styles and schools of Tai_Chi, a variety of basic exercises are executed through individual movements, the adoption of different postures, and the use of breathing and meditation exercises. These serve to teach the principles of Tai_Chi, to loosen the joints, relax the whole body and gradually modify individual posture to avoid overstressing the body's joints. Its practice consists of sequences of clearly determined fluid movements. The basic forms are individual exercises in which each practitioner performs the movements for himself, usually executed slowly and calmly, but there are a wide number of variants depending on the style, performance status and experience of the student.

Apart from training in individual movement, complete exercise sequences are carried out between two people. The fundamental principle of Tai_Chi is softness; the practitioner should move in a natural and fluid manner, relaxed at all times. There are no exercises to demonstrate strength, speed or muscle hardening. Tai_Chi is performed slowly in order to apply the techniques as correctly as possible. The three key points are:

- body relaxation;
- breathing; and
- concentration.

When exercising, the body should be what teachers of the art would describe as "in a state of sleep", such as occurs at night when we are experiencing rapid eye movements or "REM", which confirm health-restoring sleep. Only those muscles that are really needed for a certain movement or posture are tightened, whilst the rest of the body maintains a relaxed muscle tone. It is a form of relaxation that promotes the expression of the so-called "Yin" force. This is coordinated jointly in the body and is not obstructed by any type of tension.

Breathing should be deep, relaxed and flow naturally. Air needs to be drawn right down into the lower part of the lungs. Beginners, in most cases, must first learn to breathe deeply or to adapt their breathing to the pace of the exercises. Meanwhile, at a later stage of experience, the breathing rhythm displayed by advanced practitioners naturally adjusts to the exercise movements. However, the different branches of tai chi have separate ways of practising breathing, and so it is not possible to make sweeping generalisations about it. Movements must be consciously made and built up as a mental discipline. The concentration of the practitioner on the way in which his body is moving and posturing is important, but students must not forget to distribute body weight and tension evenly, hovering between the perception of personal movement and the dynamics of the environment. Movements should not only be focused but spread in intensity throughout the body. Devotees of tai chi also need to be mindful of the place they hold as part of a much bigger universe.

The ten fundamental rules of tai chi are:

- raise your head in a relaxed way;
- keep your chest straight and your back upright;
- relax the lumbar region and the waist;
- distribute weight correctly;
- let shoulders and elbows hang completely without tension;
- coordinate the top part of the body with the bottom;
- focus on harmony between the internal and the external;
- keep movements flowing uninterruptedly;
- remain calm and at peace during the exercises; and
- keep focused on the movements.

Yoga

Yoga is the name given to a set of disciplines and practices of a physical and mental nature where the objective is to achieve a balance between body and mind and a union with the Absolute (universe). As such, the word comes from the Sanskrit "yoga", which signifies "union" or "effort". The concept has two major applications, i.e. on the one hand, it is the set of physical and mental disciplines that originated in India and which seeks to achieve spiritual perfection and union with the Absolute; on the other hand, yoga is made up of practices that derive from the Hindu tradition that promotes mastery of the body and a greater ability to concentrate. In modern times, it is practised by those who strive to achieve the integration of the soul with God and by those who seek to develop their spiritual consciousness. Yoga can also be considered as a kind of physical activity that helps to improve the posture of the body. Its origin can be found in India, in the Indus valley. Its antiquity, however, is difficult to determine but its practice is thought to be between three and five thousand years old. Currently, yoga has become enormously popular in the Western world. It is seen as a discipline largely based on Hindu theories, but primarily focused on the practice of a set of techniques aimed at achieving greater control of the body and mind. Modern yoga is rather a system of exercises that enables the practitioner to achieve balance and spiritual harmony, all through meditation and a series of postural and breathing exercises. There are multiple schools and streams of yoga, which usually share the same bases. According to Hindu doctrine, the essence of a human being is the soul, which is enclosed in the body. This, in turn, can be divided into physique, mind, intelligence and ego. Today, the most widespread and practised type of yoga, especially in the West, is "hatha" yoga. It includes a sequence of postures and breathing exercises that strengthen the body and promote states of relaxation. The practice of yoga is closely linked to the exercises of "pranayama" for breathing control. Prana is the vital energy contained within our body as we breathe. Combining exercise and breathing is essential to achieve this peace of mind. Amongst its many benefits, yoga helps an individual to derive a more harmonious relationship with their body, to control his mind and emotions, as well as to liberate his mind and body of stress. All these features contribute to an overall state of greater well-being. A sense of full satisfaction in life is reached through the gratification of physical needs promoted by a healthy and active lifestyle, through psychological development, i.e. access to knowledge and power, and through spiritual awakening. Below are further, more detailed descriptions of the benefits of yoga.

Physical

Generally, the practice of yoga increases the body's energies, frees it from toxins, strengthens its natural defences against disease and tunes in to the stimuli of our environment, thereby optimising the integral functioning of the body. Yoga:

- improves the flexibility of muscles and joints, promoting vitality and agility;
- increases physical strength, exercising the muscles whilst improving the overall appearance of our body;
- streamlines the body's metabolism and aids healthy muscle building through the circulation of energy and oxygenation of the body;

- heightens the production of endorphins in the body which contribute to the control of pain and inflammation responsible for some painful physical conditions;
- is considered by many as a holistic medicine that prevents and heals chronic diseases, e.g. various researchers give assurances that the practice of yoga improves the condition of patients suffering from asthma, chronic fatigue, arthritis and arteriosclerosis, amongst other disorders;
- helps to improve breathing, which has a direct impact on the health of the body's organs as well as teaching us to make better use of energy;
- protects the integrity of the spine through the promotion of improved posture and blood flow so that the vertebrae are at less risk of deterioration;
- is seen as a natural ingredient in the fight against ageing and as a way to combat stress, returning a natural harmony to our body which is lost when we allow stress to invade our lives;
- by means of specific exercises, helps to stimulate our internal organs, producing positive results for the neurological, endocrine, digestive and respiratory systems; and
- combats the risk of high blood pressure, and, along with improving the production of anti-oxidants, aids the control of excessive cholesterol and sugar levels.

Mental exercise

Yoga:

- generates calm and sharpens the brain, giving us greater emotional and mental stability;
- is a good resource with which to fight depression;
- helps fight episodes of anger and panic; and
- improves our resistance to stress, the control of anxiety and the ability to focus attention on the important issues of day-to-day living so that we do not feel that we are drowning in problems.

Meditation

Broadly speaking, meditation refers to a type of mental exercise and personal reflection that people practise in association with something in particular, either spiritual or physical. It is an activity that can be done by anyone. Etymologically, the word "meditation" originates from the Latin "*meditatio*", which indicates the action of meditating. It encourages the practice of concentration and relaxation so that students can analyse their inner and exterior world. This allows a clearer view and a different perspective of everything they experience, including any features that may be generating uncertainty or discontent. From a religious point of view, meditation refers to the time that an individual devotes to prayer or spiritual contemplation. The idea of meditation varies according to geographical and cultural context. In the Western world, the word "meditation" refers to reflection, thinking or reasoning but in the East it has a different significance. Those who live in Europe or America, following the religious traditions of those Continents, have a different vision and understanding of meditation than those who have been brought up in the cultural and religious customs of Asia and nearby countries. In the latter areas, the practice of meditation has been of great value and importance for thousands of years. Traditionally, meditation in India has a strong link to yoga itself. In fact, in its beginnings, as can be read in Patanjali's *Yoga Sutras* (3ʳᵈ century B.C.), yoga is inextricably linked with its own brand of meditation. The ultimate goal of its practices was the union of the individual with the Absolute, or God. In Buddhism, meditation is a spiritual technique which inspires inner contemplation of our being and our environment. The aim is to recognise and better understand who we are, gain wisdom and minimise suffering both for ourselves and for others. Either way, be it a religious or therapeutic exercise of the mind, the main objective of meditation is to reach a point of concentration and mental relaxation in order to feel inner peace; after constant practice the student will start to feel the benefit.

Meditation techniques

There are several meditation techniques. The best known and practised are those that originated in India; they are revered as being the oldest. However, new practices have emerged that have also become fashionable, especially in countries in the Western world. It is important to point out that although there are different ways of meditating, all of them begin with the same principle, i.e. that of observing and analysing our thoughts from a perspective of stillness, silence and concentration.

Once the individual is in a state of complete relaxation, he tries to empty or to release himself from his thoughts. It is then that he can contemplate his emotions and feelings whilst somewhat distancing himself from them. From this, the individual becomes more aware of his own personal experiences, favouring introspection and self-knowledge.

Factors to be taken into account when meditating include:

- **Breathing**: This should be calm; inhale and exhale gently and repeatedly to feel how air enters and leaves the body.
- **Body posture:** The person who meditates should sit with his back upright, with his hands on his knees and legs crossed. Maintaining silence, breathing softly and slowly, the individual should visualise himself completely and recognise himself for what he is. People who have physical limitations do not have to cross their legs to maintain the classic lotus position. They can practise sitting as long as they keep their backs straight.
- **Eyes closed**: During the meditation process, closing your eyes and visualising everything in your mind clearly and serenely is recommended. It is important to emphasise that meditation should be practised in a comfortable space away from any situation that generates restlessness or noise.

Different types of meditation

- **Guided meditation**: This practice refers to students being guided through the process of meditation by the voice of a teacher or a specialist. The aim is to promote calm, tranquillity and inner peace which acts as a springboard from which to advance through life with safe and positive steps. Through guided meditation, people learn to listen and to focus all their attention on the precise nature of what they are being taught. The teachers and guides will lead their students to a state of inner calm that allows them to become relaxed in both body and mind. This can combat, amongst other states of mind, stress, anxiety and sleep difficulties.

- **Transcendental meditation:** This is a technique created in India by Maharishi Mahesh Yogi during the final years of the 1950s. It aims to achieve a deep form of relaxation that allows individuals to "walk" through their thoughts and experience psychological calm and physical rest.

- **Sleep meditation**: This is a type of guided meditation practised by those who suffer constant sleep difficulties. In these cases, it is not only the number of hours of sleep that need to be increased but also the quality of rest. Sleep meditation offers various techniques that people can adopt as a daily activity. So, this form of meditation encourages people to relax, breathe deeply and fall asleep. On waking, they will feel better equipped mentally and physically to face a new day.

- **Zen meditation**: This is a form of Buddhist meditation that has its origins in Japan. It is easily recognised by the traditional lotus posture that people adopt where the face and torso, during practice, face the wall. Zen meditation aims to touch people's hearts and positively change their spirits.

Chapter 8

Love and happiness

When a person hears the word "love", there is a lot that it can suggest. Its concept can be as broad or narrow as one wants to understand or feel. So, two unrelated people who experience love together do so as a couple. Separately, love can be what parents feel for their children, for their relatives, for their pets, plants, planet and universe, or it can even mean the compassion that can invade us when we think of the whole of humanity. Being something so universal and at the same time so subjective, love as a concept can be defined in many ways. As a generalisation, we refer to love as a feeling of affection and attachment that occurs because of certain attitudes, emotions or experiences. Some would specify the definition of love with a little more clarity, declaring it to be a set of feelings that occurs between human beings capable of reasoning and of having emotional and affective intelligence. It is such proponents that suggest a deep feeling that intensifies our interpersonal relationships, and which gives us a greater sense of fulfilment and completeness as people in our own right. When this happens, we put the needs or desires of the loved one before ours, leading us to care more about the other's happiness than our own. We associate love with being the expressions of affection and kindness that we give to, or receive from, others. Since the beginning of time, love's essence has inspired the creation of an endless number of works of art, philosophical writings and scientific discoveries. If we stop to reflect a little, we will realise that we are always surrounded by love, even though we are often not conscious of it. It is something that all living beings need. Both humans, animals and some would even say love for plants, falls into this category.

Not everyone may understand the love of plants and flowers. Here is an example. You walk into a house and realise how beautiful and exuberant the plants are in it. You look at the owner and watch as she takes care of them, waters them when necessary and from time to time, "speaks to them". She communicates with them, letting them know how happy she is in their presence. You will probably have noticed that there is also harmony and peace in that house. This happens because the plants are happy, filtering the air positively, creating a fresh and pleasant atmosphere. Plants are, like us, living beings who respond in their own way to our compliments. We could cite other examples, such as when someone is a little sad and takes a walk in the countryside amid abundant vegetation. After a while, it seems as if something has happened to alter your mood. Your spirits begin to lift and you begin to think positively again. Equally, if you have a pet in your home, attend to its needs and love it. You will feel happier, as if there is another element of affection in your life. The animal will sense the affection that you have for it.

The following case is scientifically proven. In Germany, there are special centres who treat people with anxiety and depression. The therapy is very simple and effective. The only work that the patients need to do is to look after a puppy. After weeks, and sometimes after months, the psychology of the people who need treatment improves greatly. We all need love, i.e. young people, children, adults, elderly people, animals and plants. We find ourselves happier and healthier with love in our lives. The problem is that sometimes we get lost along the way. We sometimes think that what we are feeling is love when in fact it may be another emotion. This frequently happens when we consider looking for or finding a partner. In this sense, the concept of love shared by a couple can be seen as a cultural construction that has changed greatly over the course of history. In Ancient Greece, for example, sexuality and sexual relations, both heterosexual and homosexual, were clearly separated from marriage. In Rome, the cultural scenario was similar. In the High Middle Ages, love, marriage and pleasure were seen as separate social engagements and totally independent of one another. Between the 16th and 18th centuries, marriages of convenience, without the need for any concept of love being present between the couple, were the norm. It was not until the 19th century that the concept of romantic love, as we know it today, emerged. Marriage, sexuality and romantic love become bonded in the feelings that a couple have for each other. Today, most people, at least in the Western world, believe that romantic love is the fundamental reason for maintaining a marital relationship and that "being in love" is the reason for forming a relationship and staying in it. However, the sociobiological conception of love is based on the functionality it has for the survival of the species. The sexual differences between men and women associated with sexual behaviour and love are based on sexual selection, i.e. the pressure that individuals of one sex exert on those of the other through competition. Men will thus prefer physical attractiveness and mutual attractiveness when choosing a partner whilst women, on the contrary, will value power and social status more when choosing a partner owing to their greater effort and investment in child-rearing. What is known as the culturalist conception, meanwhile, maintains that passionate love is a social construct that occurs only in certain cultures and at certain historical moments. However, from this point of view, and from both psychological and anthropological schools of thought, more and more people are supporting the idea that love is a universal phenomenon, although its importance may vary significantly from one cultural environment to another and even over time.

Love is normal, but being in love is not a normal situation. Those who fall in love are in a phase of transitory abnormality, as they behave in a subtly distorted way when they are "in love". They usually buy more, tend to worry more about their physical appearance and dress more stylishly. They also spend more money on the person they love. Rationally, this altered behaviour could appear bizarre. This often unconscious behaviour has the biological goal of reproduction in its sights, but this is only one perspective of so-called romantic love. One can love with great passion beyond the phase of fertility and in such cases, reproduction could never be the end goal.

In 1956, psychologist and philosopher Erich Fromm, influenced by authors of psychoanalytical and behavioural tendencies, provided an exquisite analysis of love and the practice of loving in his book "The Art of Loving". He defined love as an art in which both the theoretical and practical sides should be explored. He attached great importance to perfecting the art, applying its powerful force to a wide range of situations and people that we might meet in life. Subsequently, many authors have been inspired by his work. At the time of writing "The Art of Loving", Fromm subdivided love into several types, i.e. fraternal, maternal, erotic, of oneself and of God.

Without forgetting its great contribution, this guide, adapting to a modern era, also aimed to analyse the variants of love experienced in our daily lives, e.g. love of oneself, during childhood, in the home, romantic love between couples, the love and respect of father and son, fraternal, love during the latter part of our lives and spiritual love.

If someone wants to understand the fuller and deeper meaning of love, they should ask themselves questions such as why we always look for someone to love. Why do people also experience strong feelings of love long after the ability to produce children has passed? Why do we always need to feel loved? How do we feel if we think that no one loves us?

Love of self

First of all, as Fromm pointed out, we must mention love of "oneself". This type of affection is not interpreted as egoism but refers to the idea that we are all worthy of love, and that conscious love has to begin with our own person. Through this acknowledgement of self-worth, other individuals become the focus of unselfish love. This act, in theory, can therefore be extended to the whole of humanity. When we love a particular person, we also feel love towards ourselves. It can be viewed metaphorically as a benevolent virus affecting the whole of mankind. Love of oneself forms part of love for others since one must have experience of loving oneself in order to be able to love another in a positive and unselfish way. This aspect of love is closely related to our self-esteem.

Love in childhood

Receiving love is essential for the physical and mental health of children. People who lack love in their childhood may have serious problems adapting to society when they become adults, both emotionally and in the workplace. In fact, it can become a serious problem for psychological balance. In adulthood, such children will be prone to experiencing a void of some kind, a sense of incompleteness, often striving to find a way to satisfy this need of love that they lacked in their childhood. This frequently progresses to establishing relationships with couples, a tactic which would rarely satisfy their long-term needs. An important fact to keep in mind is that people who have been deprived of love in childhood demonstrate such behaviour unconsciously, often completely unaware that they are seeking compensation in the midst of other relationships for deprivation suffered in early life.

It is sad when an adult feels isolated, unappreciated and unloved. The fact is more serious when this happens to children. They are obviously more vulnerable because they have not yet developed intellectual capacities which will allow them to defend themselves emotionally. If we educate children lovingly, it will increase their biological and emotional defences. Children who are treated with love have a more highly developed hypothalamus, a component of the brain essential for learning and managing stress. If this is not developed at a young age, it can lead to the appearance of ongoing problems such as mental health difficulties, including the inability to cope with stress and depression. It is therefore important that childhood is full of caring, meaningful relationships in order to promote a healthy balance of intellectual and emotional maturation in adulthood. If we are one of those adults who felt that we were not loved in our childhood, we can always take the initiative and change the negative view that we have of our past; it will certainly improve our present. We can, so to speak, "toss the pancake up in the air" so that it falls down on the reverse side and perceive our past experiences differently. Although they were hard to live through, such experiences could be seen as a good grounding to prepare for the future, steeling an individual for whatever life's challenges might be.

Love At Home

We have to be realistic and practical. "LOVE ALWAYS BEGINS AT HOME". We have all been children and the fortunate amongst us will have received love from our parents, even if we sometimes do not remember it very well or took it for granted. The family makes up a home where, in addition to food, protection and rest, we enjoy mutual affection. Qualities like kindness, honesty, solidarity and responsibility need to be part of the daily routine in the home. If we consciously partake in the make-up of such harmony, it will raise our sense of self-worth, enable us to develop a strong and intelligent personality and promote natural optimism and self-motivation.

I will give some examples to underline the difference between types of behaviour in the home. If you behave like a kind, helpful and educated person, and also help with household chores, such as washing laundry or mowing the lawn, this contribution will enforce the unspoken harmony of the household. If, on the other hand, you are frequently displaying ill humour, shouting angrily and always complaining about most things, this is not a good use of love. People who behave this way often misinterpret affection, paying back genuine family kindness with ill temper. Most of us, at some stage in our earlier lives, take many things in the home for granted and expect daily tasks to be done by others. You may think that you cannot see the connection between happiness and household chores clearly. I will simply clarify it. Let us start with a simple example. In order for any machine to work perfectly, the screws and components that go to make up the whole must be well-adjusted. Well, it is the same for us as human beings. We have to contribute to shoring up the foundations of harmony and tranquillity in the home to feel good from the outset. This analysis is important. It is essential that you make it a starting point. Consider your home as the place where you spend most of your time. It is also the place where you rest and recharge your batteries to face the daily challenges of life. If, for some reason, we are not completely at ease in our home life, it will be difficult for us to find a base to re-energise ourselves at the end of each day. If there is conflict in the home, it is important to address any tensions with other members of the household. People sharing the same home need to work as a team in order to make it a place of happiness, rest and recuperation. The principle of teamwork, however, should not smother the individual contributions made by each member, nor undervalue their unique personalities. Above all, be open to the exchange of ideas and think them through with a view to adopting them for the greater good of the household. Flexibility is important. Imposing our own rules for selfish ends or the imposition of power threatens the harmony of the home. If you manage to resolve all the problems in your household and work hard in it, the contribution you make for the benefit of the common good will promote the "happiness levels" of the entire household. You should continue with this effort, not just every once in a while but rather it should be a regular feature of everyday life; it should become customary. We normally live with our immediate family members, so it is also important to create harmony for them too. Do not think of your efforts as just another job. See it as something constructive and contribute more. If some tasks are not properly mastered, such as putting on the washing machine, ironing or hanging up the clothes, do not worry as you will always find someone to help you. If you follow these recommendations, you will still have more free time than if you do nothing, as you will be making the most of your time at home. Historically, these chores have been done by women who are usually more willing and able to do them. In modern times, this has changed. Men have to acknowledge that women also work outside the home, care for the children, go shopping and, after all this, still have time for household chores, not forgetting the cooking and washing up. A woman would also like some help with these daily tasks. The working circumstances of each family and its members define the role that each member of the family takes with respect to household chores. We could conclude this section by saying that if you make sure that all the members of your family or household are in good physical and psychological health, it is like an energy that is transmitted from one to another. Little by little, you will feel better and have more energy as the quality of your night's sleep improves. Everything falls into place like a chain reaction; one thing leads to another, and so on. Everyone can help at home; age or gender is irrelevant. Let us think positively, like a sporting team who all have to work together to score!

Romantic Love

Romantic love is one of the models of love that has helped to promote monogamous marriage in modern cultures. It is an ideal that society has nurtured as a necessary boundary that should govern our lives. It is considered different from other ideals of love because it can encompass concepts such as attraction, sexual desire and pleasure. It is a generalised, but not adequately analysed human understanding to think that we desperately need it in our lives to succeed, to be well and to be happy. Many people frequently have in their mind's eye a vision of what "the perfect couple" should look like, although the reality is that it is a prefabricated idea. Once we discover that our fantasy is not reality, disillusionment can set in. In the case of romantic love, the person who is the object of desire is, to a certain degree, idealised. It is a feeling based on admiration and attraction.

Mutual attraction and admiration lead to a passionate and sexual relationship between two people that has a very important influence on our lives. This intense personal relationship involves a tacit understanding on the part of both parties that they complement one another. This state of affairs lasts a short time; the infatuation declines little by little. Sex has special relevance for the couple "in love". We will assume that sexual pleasure gives us encouragement, motivates us and makes us feel healthier both physically and psychologically, but it would be unwise to give it pride of place at the centre of our universe. A person would be ill-advised to depend on sexuality for everything. Sexuality can be a good point of support for our emotional balance, but should not replace the love that generates it, i.e. the loving emotional bond between two people. When studying the significance of romantic love, we have to start from the basic premise that men and women have been socialised differently. Since our birth, the educational system, the family, the media, the use of language and religion amongst others, have been slotting men and women into two different categories. Thus, the masculine has been socially associated with power, rationality, work and politics. In contrast, feminine imagery emphasises the importance of a private life, subordination to men, passivity, dependence and obedience. This cruelly unequal societal division eats its way into different aspects of human lives, unbalancing relationships. Men and women have been conditioned to judge who or what to fall in love with, or not, and what feelings they should or should not have. Even the meaning of who or what is attractive has been inculcated through the pressure of societal norms often led by traditional gender role patterns. Society also determines how the relationship between the couple should be, whether asymmetrical, egalitarian or otherwise. Evidently, and inevitably, we also learn all the myths about love prevailing in our culture. For women, society's dogma about what romantic love should be emerges more strongly. For them, love is, or should be, the centre of their lives around which all other issues should revolve. It is often the case that cinema, television, literature and music reinforce and nurture what some would describe as a pernicious myth. Without it, one example is that "life is completely meaningless". We should certainly question the endurance of this myth in an age which has claimed the victory of emancipation for women.

Romantic love is therefore the manifestation of love that brings more myths in its wake along with the marketing imagery that supports them, but we can be profoundly unhappy as a result. Both manifestations of love have their origin in the so-called bosom of the family. Family love enshrines a very deep-seated affection which is ushered down the generations from parents to children, grandparents to grandchildren and vice versa. Separately, fraternal love creates an intense bond between siblings. It also extends to people who may not be linked with the family, developing into a relationship between equals, e.g. with friends or colleagues at work, or between members of a team. This fraternal love, in its highest expression, is associated with the "love thy neighbour" ethos which many religions underpin, a love based on unconditional equality of need between people. In the case of fraternal love, we are taught to share our goods and to live together, setting aside selfish interests for the benefit of others in the same home or community. It prepares us to live in society and can extend to those who are not of any blood relation, but the shared love is the same as if they were. It is a universal affection. It involves a set of feelings and actions that are given selflessly and shared with all those individuals around us. In the course of human life, there are some circumstances and situations that are not the object of choice. We cannot choose our parents or the place where we are born, nor can we choose our siblings. This can bring us problems at various stages of our life. As children, there are fights amongst siblings to attract the attention of parents. As adults, there are also disputes over relationships. The most perfect brotherly love is mutual love, but this cannot be guaranteed amongst siblings. In the case of unrequited fraternal love, it can become mutual if one of the siblings begins to love the other without seeking any reward for himself. The conflict experienced in infancy or maturity can be healed through the nurturing of this fraternal love. We desire the best for a neighbour who we recognise as being equal to us in terms of needs and wants.

Regarding the love between father and son, there is always a relationship of authority and superiority and so this cannot be a love between equals as the son is subordinate to the father. Love between brothers, however, is mutual recognition of equality within the family. Siblings have the capacity to wish each other well more sincerely because they see in the other a reflection of themselves. Hence, fraternal love fosters feelings as noble as affection, respect, humility, trust, esteem, loyalty and compassion. Such love should be treasured and honoured as an important aspect of human existence.

Love in old age

Love is something which has always been part of our lives since birth and which will be ever-present throughout our lives. It does not matter where we were born, where we live, or what culture or religion we follow. To fall in love, or to fall in love again in the latter part of life, is something wonderful which can fill our whole being with happiness. At such an age, we no longer pay so much attention to the physical, but rather to the person himself or herself. It is akin to a universal awareness of existence. Owing to a newly found loving relationship, we feel safer and more protected. It rejuvenates us physically and mentally. Sometimes our children or relatives may react unfavourably to us finding a new partner later in life. If this should happen, we have to take the approach that the distaste of people close to us is simply their problem. We must listen to our hearts, no matter how old we are. We can always love as long as we exist. We come to realise that falling in love is not exactly the same as loving. At a later stage in life, we have already lived through many experiences. Older people value feeling loved rather than other aspects of the feeling that would apply, for example, to romantic love. So, whilst we can fall in love at any age, it is also true that we can feel love without falling in love. In old age, it is very satisfying for people to feel loved by family, neighbours, friends or even by carers at a residential home. I was personally witness to this during a period of time I spent working as an intern in a residential care home, taking care of an elderly couple. It was a bittersweet experience. Giving support to the couple filled me with happiness on the one hand, whilst at the same time, the situation was tinged with sadness. Some of those older people at the residential home had previously had large and successful businesses, and even a lot of social power, but now they were ending their days, sometimes sad and alone. Their children or relatives visited them infrequently, perhaps once or twice a month.

For dependent, elderly people, feeling valued by someone is most essential. The things that are important to young and middle-aged people such as money, material possessions or intimate relationships, now become secondary. The first thing for older people is the health and the esteem of their nearest and dearest. We will end this section with a sentence that I have always found very beautiful, i.e. "being someone's first love is wonderful, but being the last is unsurpassable."

Spiritual love

Spiritual love is global. It is in everything and everyone, but we have to seek to find it. It is love in capital letters, unconditional, no matter what underpins it. We all have the seed to develop this within us, especially if we practise spiritual exercises. The path to spiritual love develops our consciousness and awareness of the world around us. It is not an easy path to tread. It is a constant task of exploring self-knowledge built up over a lifetime. Such awareness can bring a global change to our lives in the broadest sense, i.e. physical, spiritual and psychological. The development of our spiritual self will trigger the growth of our wider consciousness, well outside of our local, comfort zone. We will feel healthier, more fulfilled and freer. This type of love produces a radical, profound change in the lives of those who experience it. Spiritual love entails an authentic transformation of the being that is totally illuminating, bringing with it total peace. Its ideal is not only the fusion of our psychological and physical self, but the promotion of our understanding of life itself. Western and Middle Eastern beliefs speak of "closeness to God" whilst some religions, originating in the East, would talk of "enlightenment". Not everyone who embarks on this path to spiritual enlightenment will reach the goal. Others may not reach full enlightenment but will certainly have many "light bulbs" in their minds about who they are, and what role they play in creation. This does not mean that we should all lead the life of a hermit, but if we are able to control our obsession with material acquisition and avoid worrying about inconsequential matters, it is a starting block for the liberation of our soul and consciousness. The expansion of our minds is the means by which to achieve the goal of spiritual, environmental and global love.

Love is an eternal process of the mysteries of the infinite that can fill our hearts completely. We can experience happiness through helping other human beings who we hardly know just by recognising that they are in need. The first steps to enable the development of spiritual love are:

- our minds must remain relaxed, in a state of calm and peace;
- dispel negative and disturbing thoughts;
- remain strong-willed and determined;
- do not come into conflict with others on a regular basis;
- meditate normally;
- love all things equally;
- love all beings equally; and
- become aware of the power of our own psyche or consciousness.

Chapter 9

I can be my own guide

Up until now, we have observed, analysed and become aware of our situation. At this point in the guide, we already know that we want to move forwards towards happiness, not to a fleeting or pleasant contentment, but to a kind of true feeling that goes much further, one that is evidently something permanent and which makes us feel connected with ourselves and with the rest of the world. At this stage, we will have realised the need to act now and to not let another minute pass in a state of unhappiness or dissatisfaction, or in the inertia of a comfortable life void of incentives. We have begun to train ourselves; we have learned to identify and detect the negative ideas that harass us. We will also have managed to establish a series of healthy habits to keep us in good physical and psychological shape. It is much easier to achieve happiness if you are a healthy person. In the meantime, we have been able to reflect on what love, in its many forms, brings to our lives, how important its presence is in our daily existence and how it affects our own actions. It is not possible to experience life in all its fullness without understanding, giving and receiving love, whatever shape it may take. Now, we pause along the way to assume that in order to be happy, one has to take risks. To take action, yes, but where do I start? With one's own happiness at stake, the most logical and easiest thing would be to start with oneself. In essence, all people are able to develop wisdom from birth. The challenge is to recover that unconscious knowledge that we all have within us. The idea of being our own teacher or our own guide is therefore not difficult. Now, we are sufficiently motivated and encouraged to work our way towards happiness. Our training has already started and continues through the chapter.

Our own image: how we see ourselves

Next, we will analyse, subjectively and logically, some aspects of ourselves. Although they seem to be simple questions, not so many people have asked them of themselves. The great majority of us remain in ignorance about what we are really like, either internally or externally. This lack of self-knowledge is sometimes a result of pure unconsciousness and neglect, or because we inflate our ego with mistaken ideas, many of them inherited from our closest family environment.

We will start with some simple questions. Write the answers in your notebook and make a note of the date.

- Who and what are you?
- Who do you want to become and what do you want to become?
- Do you find yourself attractive?

We can ask these questions at any time and in any situation. It does not matter what age you are or what your circumstances are. It is never too late to start. Think of yourself as being as attractive as you think you are. If you have low self-esteem, this will inevitably be an obstacle lying across the path to happiness. You have to tap into your personal magnetism. Once you have taken a good long look at yourself, what you see, in all honesty, will form the basis for honing your finer points and phasing out the less good. What is clear is that you can no longer reject the person you are. It is important to learn to look good, and to take advantage of both your inner and outer self. Whilst it is true that not everyone can have a totally svelte figure with a body similar to professional models, there is always room for improvement. We can dress up more, clothe ourselves smartly, which is **not** synonymous with dressing expensively, and in general, take care of our physical appearance a little more. Our appearance reveals much about ourselves. If we take care of these details, it will have a direct impact on how we go about our daily lives. If we improve our exterior self, we will surely love ourselves a little more and this will have a knock-on effect on our inner lives.

Going along just fine

Dressed well, clean, cared for, in good shape within our limits and leading a healthy life is the springboard from which to influence deeper aspects of our lives. Deep down, it is so easy that you will ask yourself how it is possible that "you did not realise all this before." Well, a logical explanation is that most of us are so immersed in day-to-day routine and also bogged down by thoughts embedded in the past that we leave little room to welcome positive change. Working to improve our external self may seem superficial, but it is really the first step to "accepting myself as I am" in order to get ready for a change for the better. I first have to take a good look at myself, to be realistic and to acknowledge my virtues and defects. My widened sense of awareness will help to bring the positive side of me to the fore and to dampen down the negative, and to help me make the best use of myself, i.e. of what is good and what is not so good. Knowing how to choose which path to take is very important. If we want to "repackage" our self-presentation both to ourselves and others, we have to "go for it". The same could be said for other dreams that we might have such as finding a partner to share our lives with, of having good friends or a job we like. The self-esteem gained from this "acceptance of self" will be the first step from which to feel motivated to seek out our destiny, which is happiness. With enthusiasm and passion, things work out better for us. Most of us have the ability to make choices in life, and this in itself is one good reason why we should feel happy.

Many people find it hard to make up their minds. If we have to choose what is best for us, we may worry about what happens if we make a mistake. Sometimes we get stuck, not knowing which is the best option, thinking that we may make the wrong decision and fearing failure. This is a somewhat negative approach; to make a mistake is human. Our mistakes can become important lessons. In addition, if we make the wrong decision, then we have the opportunity to acknowledge and to rectify it. If this proves impossible, we can try to make important changes to improve the situation. Our development as people and our growth are the result of our choices, successes and mistakes, but above all of the consciousness that produces it all. I will remind you of something important that we should all know, but only some of us are aware of it. We come into this world alone and we will leave it alone too, taking nothing with us. That is why we should try to be well, to accept ourselves as we are and to love ourselves. This is to live well in a moderate way in everything. That is not an excuse to try and satisfy our every whim. Vice and debauchery are frequently signals that perpetrators have deeply disturbing difficulties in their lives, and evidence, perhaps, that they want to avoid a situation for which, either consciously or unconsciously, no solution is seen, and therefore they seek refuge in pleasure for pleasure's sake.

Be sure to choose the best path in life and not seek satisfaction in momentary whims. Fight for your happiness and well-being in all respects. The world in which you live now is the one your consciousness has created. Our daily thoughts and ideas determine the circumstances that occur in life and create the environment in which we live.

"It's all in the mind": working with ideas

It is very important to be aware of and be responsible for our thoughts, both positive and negative. You may wonder why the reason for the analysis of both is necessary. Positive thoughts are more comfortable and easier to analyse. So, why do I also have to consider negative ones? This reasoning seems somewhat contradictory to that which has been explained so far. However, the answer is extremely simple. Positive thoughts serve to motivate us at all times in life. Once we are aware of disturbing negative tendencies or perceptions, it is best to dispel them. In previous chapters, we have explained that negative ideas can be extremely harmful. They prevent us from progressing in life. You may wonder "if I can't eliminate negative ideas and they keep going round in my head, what do I do with them?" It is true that many times they come to mind; this is more than clear. Sometimes the spiral of negativity is such that we lose sight of the fact that there is an underlying problem that urgently needs to be resolved. So what is the right approach? Once we actively recognise that these negative thoughts threaten us, we can deem them simply not worthy of consideration. We will just take note and let them go out the same way that they came in. After some practice in the exercise of "letting go of negative ideas", it will become easier and easier to achieve and we will reach a point where a particular idea will no longer perturb us. By stripping the idea of the disturbing emotion that it produces in us, it will become like an empty shell without any power over us. By ignoring the negative undercurrent, we will have eliminated it. Another way to confront the negative idea is to replace it with a positive one. It is therefore extremely important to be aware of and responsible for our thoughts and everything that is in the database of our consciousness. At first, it may be difficult for us to perform this mental exercise, but after practising consistently for some time, it will be much easier to handle.

Concentration and energy flow

When we have been training our minds for a few weeks using an ebb and flow of new ideas, we will begin to notice the first effects. By extracting negative and damaging thought processes, it will be as though we have thrown off a great weight. We will feel more alive and inspired. Our concentration will increase considerably to our own benefit. We will pay attention to the here and now. Our senses will focus on what we are doing at any particular moment. When the information that enters our mind is consistent with our goals, it is at this point that psychic energy flows effortlessly. In such an instance, there is no concern about anything. We enjoy every moment of what we are doing. Nothing distracts us; all our senses are concentrated on a single objective. There is a school of thought suggesting that any intense sensation involves this flow of psychic energy. We tend to believe that happiness is to experience pleasure, e.g. food, sex or television, but these are only ideas that we wrongly associate with emotions, ones which we believe will make us happy. On the contrary, happiness is found elsewhere. Everything in our lives has to be focused on being well, on being happy and on helping others. When a person has consistently practised experiencing this positive energy flow, their quality of life inevitably improves. Imagine an everyday situation. Many people get bored at work. Either the job is too easy, or they may not have the capability to carry out what needs to be done; there is no perfect job. Many employees feel victimised by their work environment. They convince themselves that they do not like it, but when they get home their sense of dissatisfaction becomes even worse. Feeling that they have not achieved anything, frustration and boredom create tetchiness and ill-humour, a state of affairs that becomes even more accentuated once the weekend arrives. As their daily activity decreases, people notice their sense of emptiness much more, i.e. a life without motivation of any kind, with no future projects and nothing significant to do. This would be an example where there is no energy flow at all.

If we want to be a good guide to ourselves, we need to dig deeper without delay. There has been a theme running through the contents of this book as if it were a palpable thread. Expressions such as "becoming aware" or "realising", have been appearing in one way or another throughout the chapters. Thanks to our consciousness, we know when something is not working in our lives, but it also makes us appreciate our existence on Earth in all its aspects. When we are conscious, we are also more awake because we come to realise the things that are happening to us internally, externally and environmentally.

The origin of the word "consciousness" comes from the Latin "conscientia", which means "to be aware of it". It is defined as the immediate knowledge that people have of their own existence, their environment, their actions and their reflections. Since we are rational human beings, this concept has led headlong into philosophical and scientific research, so much so that it has inspired a multitude of definitions of the word "consciousness". This is an abstraction that commonly relates to identity, mind, brain or even the entire universe. Some definitions refer to the neurological structures in the brain which house our capacity for memory. Others identify the word as being a neurological "store", where the information of the events that happen to us every day is kept. Consciousness is routinely linked with the mind and finite, rather than infinite, cerebral activity. Our nervous system determines the amount of information that we can process; this is about 126 bytes in the form of sound, visual stimuli or emotions. As we cannot embrace everything, we have to make a sensible choice about the information we want to store in order to use it properly. The point is of great importance, because according to the psychologist Mihaly Csikszentmihalyi, "everything that we see, feel and desire can be used and manipulated in our consciousness". Certainly, we can use what we perceive and interpret from the outside in order to grow as people and thus achieve a fuller and happier existence. Thus, consciousness can allow us to be happy even if the external environment is quite the opposite. The fewer the options, the easier it is to achieve harmony. Desires become simple and we settle for less. We cannot try to pretend to be what we are not. Being ourselves will put us on the road to happiness.

Reality is complex, and owing to the nature of our consciousness, it is important to control what goes in and what we leave out, so much so that it determines the content and quality of our lives. "We become aware" so that we can then act coherently and make changes in our lives to create positive energy flow.

Exercise

Sit or lie down, relaxed, without noise, music or too much light. Close your eyes and relax for 5-10 minutes. Now, visualise in your mind an object that you like, e.g. a painting, an apple or a car. Try to feel the pleasant sensations produced by these images as if you had them in front of your eyes. Contemplate yourself in a moment of total happiness. Feel the energy flow and allow it to give you internal peace.

Exercise

Try to visualise a place where you feel at ease, relaxed and totally calm with the company of your choice. Try to immerse yourself in the tranquillity of that "here and now" for about 15 minutes. You need to get to experience a sense of well-being and peace. It is important that when you can, you practise these exercises to charge yourself with positive energy. After periods of practice, you will start to realise that you no longer pay attention to simple things that previously concerned you, and that almost always, you have a greater sense of calm.

The day will come when we will be able to control our thoughts and motivate ourselves. As you can see, the exercises described in the book are more important than they seem. Do not be lazy about doing them. The benefits far outweigh the small effort that is required. If you do not have much time, you can devote about 20 minutes to it a day, i.e. day in, day out or three days a week as you see fit. At no time should you feel pressured to do them. Write down your feelings in the notebook when you are inspired. Everything has to come naturally with no rush; take your time and the benefits will appear of their own accord.

Solitude and the master that we carry inside

In general, it is better to be in contact with others than to be alone. San Juan de la Cruz, Spanish poet, theologian and mystic wrote that "solitude is the most wonderful thing". However, for most people, it is not such a good thing. You have to learn to distinguish between loneliness and being alone, and how to learn to appreciate being alone. Constant solitude can lead to becoming depressed. You may wonder why. As we have already pointed out previously, activities and daily routine can mask the things that are really important for our growth. We submerge nagging problems in the practicalities of day to day living. At first, being alone can make us feel more uncomfortable, dissatisfied and even more frustrated than we had done previously. This is where we need to be strong and patient. Being alone can help us to become our own companion, and to come to know our essential being. Silence and introspection will help "our teacher" or "our guide" to come to light and to develop. As the days pass and we practise the guidelines explained throughout this book, the quality of life will improve. Every day will be a little happier and a little more relieved.

Then, we will be able to make a more positive contribution to society and engage with others at a level that is enriching for both parties. Solitude helps us to put our ideas in order. It helps us to clarify what we want to achieve in life. Once again, here is the question of becoming aware. Now that we are more focused and relaxed, we can offer those around us the best of ourselves, with a more qualitative "presence". Life is precious and we deserve to have a heightened sense of fulfilment. Alternating periods of solitude with coexistence in society is very healthy. It is a bit like a racing car making its way through the maintenance engineer's workshop for a general overhaul prior to a competition. In the same way, we, in solitude, become aware of ourselves, i.e. of our situation before taking action and before interacting with life.

Chapter 10

A shortcut to happiness

Normally, when we talk about a "shortcut", it means that we are deciding on the shortest way to get to a place, rejecting the usual and in general, much longer route. It also refers to going to meet something or someone. In the etymology of this word, from the Latin "taliare", we can glimpse another aspect of its quite interesting interpretation, i.e. to cut the excess branches of a tree. This highly interesting derivation can serve as an example to fine-tune our attitude to achieving happiness. We try tirelessly to reach our goal and to shorten the path towards it. Shortcuts, although they lessen the length of the route, usually involve much more effort because we pass through less familiar territory where, perhaps, we have to cut branches that bar our way or to move stones out of the path, all to be able to rejoin the main road to our destination. It is necessary to act intelligently in order to develop the necessary skills to stop and to discover our own way. With practice, we will learn to overcome obstacles. Our motivation will come in the form of setting limited objectives that we will need to achieve sequentially. Having reached this stage, happiness is just around the corner. All people, although essentially the same, are different. Our birth and environment, e.g. family, education and diverse experiences, have shaped, in some form or other, our way of being. With all our defects and virtues, we are the result of our interaction with the world. Although this book was conceived from the beginning as a kind of guide to attain happiness with concrete steps to follow, the truth is that the interaction of your personality with the environment undoubtedly defines your path to follow. It will surely be different from that of other people who have followed the same quest for enlightenment. Being your own guide will show you the path to follow in this final journey towards happiness. Take courage!

Ourselves and the world around us

Most of us complain at some time or other about almost everything, e.g. the workplace, co-workers, bosses, friends who do not value us sufficiently, the couple next door who do not help things too much, the corner supermarket vendor who is not at all nice and so many other negative ideas about daily life. These are just a few examples. We do not realise it, but we always want things to happen the way that we want them to and when we want them to. We have to start being realistic and accept that there are just some things that happen around us that are out of our control. This point is important to remember, as it will ward off frustration. We cannot behave like babies or whimsical children who cry for the things they want and who are always asking for new things. If we want to become emotionally balanced, we cannot allow what happens around us to affect or to depress us. We already know that we cannot change events, but we can and must change the way that these events affect our feelings and emotions, be they sadness or sometimes frustration. When you have learned to be yourself and to accept everything that happens around you, then you will be able to say that you have strong emotional pillars and thus be closer to your goal of being happy. Sometimes, people may feel very disappointed that they have not achieved their goals in life. Perhaps you are angry with yourself because you are already of a mature age and have not got the job of your dreams, or do not have the partner and/or family you would like. You may also retain certain ideals of youth and feel resentful that you are not living in the that you had dreamed of at the time. These are just a few of many examples. It is out of the question; we simply cannot continue with that approach. I can have wonderful ideas and great projects, and every day I regret not having achieved them. However, if I do nothing to achieve my goals or projects, or I do not strive for anything, I will continue to be sorry about it every day, over and over again. As you can see, this is meaningless, because if a person wants to achieve something, whatever it is, it is obviously something that has to be fought for. Some action needs to be taken to achieve the end in mind.

The right thing would be to get down to work and to draw up a reasoned and logical plan for it. At first glance, this may seem complicated and tiring, but it is not so. In the long run, it is one of the most viable steps to follow to achieve your goals. Another important factor to bear in mind is that you have to accept the decisions of others, be they co-workers, friends or family, even though in some cases they may be contrary to your own. By compromising, we will avoid conflict and argument. After all, they are only different ideas to already accepted ones.

Imagine that you have an office colleague and he decides to change jobs. No matter how much you dislike it, the decision is the other person's right and it has to be accepted. The same thing happens if a son or daughter decides not to go to college or to marry someone you do not think is the right person for them. I could go on with more examples, but these simple ones offer you a general idea. Bear in mind that if you accept the decisions of others in instances where they have the right to make them, things will be less stressful for you. Perhaps today, most people think materialistically when it comes to being happy. I have to "have" to be happy, e.g. a plasma television, a big kitchen, a powerful, expensive car, a big house with a garden and, even better, with a swimming pool. I can tell you that basically, all this is unnecessary. It is statistically proven; there are people who have won large amounts of money on the lottery or other types of prizes, but after a few months of euphoria, the problems that they had before the financial windfall return. Sometimes, even after spending their winnings in their entirety, large debts can become a problem. We are now going to think of a moderate and logical way of achieving happiness, and for this we will resort to a very common example. Let us suppose that we have a selection of mathematical variables and coefficients to apply to different equations. To look at each one in turn, we will have to examine the equations separately, and then write them off one by one. With happiness, something similar happens. We need to think of different kinds of happiness, or rather different things that we believe can make us happy. It is now about defining and refining our goals. We do not need to be simplistic and reduce everything to having health, money and love. These are generalisations that do not reflect reality. Sometimes, simple things can make us happy. However, it can be that seeing people who are happy, at least in outward appearance, plunges us deeper into misery. We feel morally low because we think that we are not as happy as some others around us. We have already pointed out that apart from being a negative idea, the assumption is probably a superficial one which fails to correspond to reality. We have to start with ourselves, i.e. with our own ego in order to change a situation for the better. The environment can act as a stimulus for us to "get our act together", to prompt us to respond, to grow, to improve and ultimately, to be happy. The stimulus, however, will never come from the external, but rather from our inner attitude to the world around us. Few of us accept our emotional fragility. Something fundamental about happiness is to have control of our emotions and feelings. Things are really as they are rather than as we would like them to be. It is more important that although we might need to acknowledge adverse experiences that have happened to us, we should also acknowledge that they do not have to stand in the way of our ultimate happiness.

Accepting and interacting with reality

We have already worked with our "I" and ego. Ego and "I" have courageously looked at each other face-to-face, we

113

have considered who and what we are, and what we want to become. At this stage, we have accepted ourselves and all our virtues and defects with the aim of being able to use them to make the most of ourselves. Ego and "I" may already have started to love each other a little more. We have the highest self-esteem. Now it is about applying the skills used to achieve the same in external reality, i.e. in the world around us. Internally, we have accepted the person who we are, and now we will do the same externally as we move forward in life. I will give a true example. I met a gentleman in London at one of the end of year chess tournaments. In his youth, Peter was a man of medium height, with blonde hair and blue eyes; he possessed an open and enterprising mind. His father was a salesman in a small supermarket and his mother was a dressmaker in a clothing store. Both parents wanted the young Peter to study at university so that he could carve out a profitable future for himself and "be someone" in life. My friend convinced himself that once he finished college he would get a good job so that he would have more opportunities to start "a family" and "be happy". He decided to study economics at the University of London. After five years of studying and many financial sacrifices, such as not going to parties or "splashing out" at weekends, he finally graduated. He only had one hobby, chess. As long as they did not coincide with exam times, he played in all the university chess championships and in others, elsewhere in London.

For months, Peter looked for work related to what he had studied, but time passed and he could not find anything appropriate. Eventually, he had to take part in competitive professional teaching examinations and secured a place as a teacher in a high school in a small town in the south of England, quite a distance away from London. This was not a very well-paid job. In fact, it was not what he wanted, but he adapted to the situation. Over time, he expanded his social and cultural environment. He found time to work in various places, helping some of his friends with their small business enterprises for which they paid him a modest sum. Eventually, he earned more with these piece-meal jobs than he did as a teacher. Peter's story is an example of someone setting out on a professional journey and not finding what he or she really wanted at the outset. In Peter's case, by changing tack and working as an economist in more than one company, he assumed a different "external reality" with all its pros and cons, and ended up working in businesses in a way he had not foreseen, i.e. taking professional teaching examinations and using his knowledge of economics to help his friends with their business accounting. The first thing that can be deduced from all of this is that Peter learned to be satisfied with what he had, a reality that perhaps he "sadly" resigned himself to. However, if we go a little further we will see that there is much more than just the face value of this adjustment. In this exercise of "accepting reality" on the one hand, and of "renouncing" his first idea of being an economist on the other, Peter had to develop skills that made him grow as a person. Thanks to having interacted with "his reality" in such a positive way, "other doors" were opened to him. Although he did not get what he wanted at first, by following other paths he managed to gain unforeseen success in different fields which could equally bring him the satisfaction he sought. What had happened to solve the problem? As already explained, when we absorb information and it matches our objectives, psychic energy flows rapidly. My friend strived to move forward and concentrated fully on "his reality" in the "here and now". As a result, he gained something much more important than a job itself; he took advantage of his experiences and of course, learned how to live life to the full. Unlike others, Peter probably now knows how to give much more value to everything he possesses.

Sometimes, people are not entirely happy and do not know the reason why. To solve this enigma, we will ask ourselves some questions about issues that most of us take for granted and which we frequently undervalue.

You can write the answers in your workbook.

- Am I in good health?
- Do I like my work?
- Does my family provide a loving home?
- Do I have good friends?

I limit myself to mentioning just a few cases as not everyone has the same priorities in life. What for some may be exciting and enjoyable, for others may be uninteresting. Although they might appear obvious, these questions are often overlooked. However, they are important enough to impact on each of us at a profound level. As mentioned previously, we frequently hanker after material possessions, e.g. a nice large property or an expensive car, all provided by a well-paid job. When alone with our thoughts in a quiet moment, we can ask ourselves whether we really need an increasing number of material possessions to be happy.

Coming to terms with our own reality and valuing more both the material and non-material things that we already have, our stress levels will decrease and we can begin to enjoy peace of mind, an essential phase for completing our journey towards happiness. Like all shortcuts, when we have been through them frequently, they become easier to negotiate. We have already learned to remove the branches and rocks that present obstacles along the way, i.e. to use and to enhance our skills in order to achieve our goals.

The following paragraphs contain some important guidelines on preparing for and attaining happiness, which have appeared throughout this book. We need to work on our own interior, but it is easier and more successful if we are in good physical condition at the outset. It is essential to avoid extremes of being too fat or too thin. Ask your general practitioner's advice on exercise and dietary regimes. That does not mean that you should become discouraged because you are not as athletic as you think you should be. Athletes devote hours every day to fine-tuning their skills, and in most cases would have a personal trainer. We do not have the time or the money. Exercise in moderation is advisable, but it is important to get started now rather than postpone the effort for "another day".

Try not to suffer on a daily basis from past mistakes

That is easier said than done, you might say. Constant regret about something that has happened in the past will not help us to find a solution to moving forwards to happiness in the present day. We tend to blame our tension and lack of concentration on "stress" or "nerves". The following excuse is typical, i.e. "I can't learn anything. I'm feeling on edge." It is perhaps helpful to know that stress can be helpful in limited doses. Having to meet deadlines, whether in sport, the workplace or household, generates a measure of stress. The responsibility of "getting things done on time" whether it be for ourselves or others, galvanises us into action. As long as this does not involve excessive multi-tasking, there is little harm in the natural production of some adrenaline.

It is important to feel that we have stability in order to be happy. Tranquillity and the ability to relax are major supporters of a stable existence. Stability can be undermined by lack of friendships, indifference on the part of others, being undervalued in the workplace, feeling unloved by family and excessive loneliness (as opposed to aloneness, which we have already addressed as a separate state of mind). Poor self-esteem can make us believe that we "should be better than we are"; we may worry about what others think of us. It is similar to trying to see ourselves with other people's eyes and to judge our self-esteem with other people's self-esteem. In other words, the behaviour of others towards us has a disproportionate influence about whether we are feeling "good" or "bad". Negative remarks can affect us for an entire day, if not longer, depending on the context. Meanwhile, praise from those we respect and love can instil great happiness.

To be ourselves, our achievements, successes and failures should belong to us. As already discussed, the influence of people around us on our thoughts and values as we go through life is so incisive that we take their ideas as our own, but they are not. If someone wants or has a particular material possession, we assume that we should aim to have the item as well. Most people do not think of themselves as rich, possibly because we do not have a benchmark for what being rich is, or because we believe that we are deprived of something that in fact we do not really need. Feeling "rich" is a relative concept. Native peoples in South America may have plenty of gold hidden away, but if they do not go hunting they will not eat. Paradoxically, there is the example of someone who has a good job running several companies. He or she has houses rented out, but when the question "do you feel rich?" is put to them, a typical reply would be "no, not even close to it. I have to pay a lot of tax, I have to run several cars and pay for insurance, not to mention how much holidays to the Caribbean cost me each year!"

Real wealth is to be satisfied with what we already have and not to feel that we are less equal than others who might have more material possessions than ourselves.

Chapter 11

Can happiness be measured?

During your reading of "Happiness in the 21st Century", I accompanied you on a journey that I hope has been useful to you. If as yet you have not attained full happiness, then at least to have become aware of your own situation and to want to make the most of your life, which is so precious and unique, is paramount. There is still time to be spurred on to the final goal of true happiness. Is it possible at this stage to know if we have improved our lot? Are we happier than we were before we started reading this book? For you, where is happiness to be found? Have you found what you were hoping for, and what you were looking for? Throughout the course of this book, you have been given guidelines to test whether you are happy or not. We have urged you to absorb them in order to encourage you to act here and now and to fight for the fulfilment of your existence. You have been guided through the process of thought transformation, i.e. of avoiding or substituting negative ideas. We have also reviewed the good practices which are necessary to prepare the ground for getting into shape physically and mentally in order to find the best path to follow through life. I want to think that, at this point, you have already taken control of your life and have set out with determination, strength and ability on the last stretch of your journey. Many different things may have been experienced along the way. Perhaps, many of you have achieved the great goal that we sought from the beginning, i.e. happiness. Many may also have achieved permanent fulfilment. However, as we have also learned, happiness comes in different shapes and sizes, as varied as the number of people who might have read this work. You may notice the effects immediately, but it is more than likely that you will soon realise that you already want a little more, that you are beginning to be aware of details in your life that you had not previously appreciated, and that you can already glimpse something ahead of you that could prevent you from being happy and which needs resolving. Above all, you can see that you are starting to interact with the outside world in a very different way than you have done until now.

Treading the path to happiness takes tremendous personal effort, because after having resolved to leave an unfulfilling life behind, the traveller has had to identify and to root out obstacles along the way. This may have been done at significant personal cost. Previously held negative ideas would have loomed up in front of us to prevent us from seeing the light. Our work has been like peeling an onion. We have removed the outer layers in order to finally discover our true nature. After having read the book and having allowed a short time to pass, if you sense a feeling of inner peace and life takes on an ordered, meaningful pace, then surely the effort you have made has been worthwhile. Now, go back in time and remember what your personal psychology was like before starting your journey. You may have found the theory a little tedious, or you may have found it very difficult to practise the exercises. There are many pitfalls that you may have encountered before reaching this stage, but it is no less true that by overcoming them, one after another, you will have regained your lost, essential self and will feel prepared to be happy. You may even have come to the point of beginning to have fun along the way. If this happens to you, you are surely very close to your final destination.

The Barometer of Happiness

What would be the barometer of happiness? Let us make that a little more specific. Let us return to the initial idea. How can we know if we have really made progress, especially if, at an intermediate level, we have not yet reached a total sense of fulfilment? In other words, in that phase of transition where we notice how our life is changing, we need to diagnose any remaining problem at an early stage in order to successfully eliminate it. We become aware not only of the obstacle but also of the lesson behind it and what we must learn in order to progress. If we are still aware of the degree to which we have advanced, we could measure happiness as the pressure on a barometer or the temperature on a thermometer. In the highest and most positive measurements, we would find those related to happiness such as joy, empathy with others, enthusiasm, constructive thoughts, relaxation, peace, tranquillity and calm. In measurements reflecting the lowest negative values, the list would include melancholy, anger, sadness, stress, anxiety, depression, unhappiness, continuous pessimism and mental instability.

An exercise here could be:

Draw a thermometer or barometer with positive and negative numbers. Then, mark the level we feel we have reached with a pen. Although it may be evident that we have made little progress, it is very important to measure it correctly and honestly. You can repeat this exercise when you need to, even if it is a while since you finished reading the book. The results can reflect quite relative values and, from one reader to another, can vary considerably. It does not matter as it is only a reference that can serve as a guide.

Let us recap!

Once we know approximately what stage we have reached, it is important to specify which parts of the practice of this book have been simple and which have been more complicated. At this point, it is a question of doing a self-analysis of your interaction with the study of this book. Which practices and exercises have you easily managed? Which exercises have you not been able to do at all? Which ones have been more difficult than others? The assumption is made that if you have reached this point, it is because you have finished reading this work, but it is also possible that you may have wanted to abandon it on more than one occasion. Why? In which sections have you got stuck or felt that there was not a way forward? All this can make us more aware of the reason why we have only advanced to a certain point, or why, on the contrary, it has been easy for us to reach the final or even the reason why we have managed to attain complete happiness. This analysis proposes a list of questions that you must write down in your notebook. It is not a test to correct or to list your successes. This is more an exercise of reflection and summing-up that will allow you to self-evaluate and to take stock of what you have achieved. It is also an opportunity to "measure" the point you have reached and to focus on aspects you still have to work on and to improve.

1. Was it difficult for you to start reading this book? Think about your answer.
2. Consider and write down whether or not you were happy before starting to read the book.
3. Remember three happy moments in your life and relate them to an emotion and a motive.
4. How many happy events in your life are linked to money? In the event of there being several examples of these, write down the ultimate motive of what generated each happiness.
5. On a scale of 1 to 10, try to imagine what degree of happiness you enjoyed at the start of your reading of "Happiness in the 21st century". Write down your answer.
6. Did you have a difficult time deciding to fight for your happiness?
7. How long did it take from the time you made the decision until you actually started working on it?

8. Consider what obstacles prevented you from moving forward at first.

9. When you did the relaxation and meditation exercises, did all sorts of thoughts enter your mind? Were most of them positive or negative?

10. Replace negative ideas with positive ones or let negative thoughts pass. What did you experience when you first did these exercises? Was it difficult or easy for you?

11. After some time of practising how to reshape your way of thinking, did you experience improvement in your mood and/or an increase in your ability to concentrate? Did your stress or anxiety levels decrease?

12. Did doing moderate physical exercise or practising some of the disciplines outlined, such as tai chi, yoga or Pilates help you to feel better?

13. Have you managed to include healthy practices as part of your everyday life? Think about your answer and consider what obstacles you have encountered.

14. Think about your relationships with loved ones and the ones you have with friends. Are these relationships really what you think they are? Did you expect more of these? What misconceptions did you realise you had about your family, partner or friends?

15. Have you come to see truthfully what **you** are really like? Have you accepted yourself as you are, with all your virtues and defects?

16. Have you begun to work with your ideas? Have you been able to experience and enjoy concentration and thought flow?

17. When you are really at peace with yourself, do you feel alone?

18. Are you aware of and do you accept your surroundings, e.g. environmental, social, cultural and professional? Have you learned to interact with your own reality?

19. Are you beginning to feel that you are "yourself"?

20. Do you sense or even already see what "your path" is in life, at this very moment?

21. Having finished reading the book, on a scale of 1 to 10, how far do you think you have advanced along your path to happiness?

22. Generally speaking, what has been the greatest obstacle to being able to read and to practise the philosophy of this work?

23. Do you feel happier now?

The answers to these questions can help to give you an idea of how far you have come. Even if you think you still have a long way to go, remember that you have already taken a big step. You have become aware of the reality of your own individual situation and lifestyle and you want to improve it. You may need more or perhaps less time to achieve your goal but now, unlike before, you are on your way. You are on the threshold of a fuller existence and of the blossoming of your true self.

Obstacles along the way

To become happy is the final destination, but, as in any great journey, we will probably encounter some obstacles along the way. There is the danger that we will be tempted to abandon the trip. This could happen at any point, e.g. at the outset of the journey or at a later stage, after we have immersed ourselves in further chapters of the book. However, if we treat these obstacles as a challenge, as an opportunity to learn and become stronger mentally and physically, we have the opportunity to take the final leap and to transform our lifestyles into ones that provide us with the peace and happiness that we seek. The process will sharpen our skills and raise awareness not just of our own capabilities but of the world around us.

The first great obstacle that can appear in the way is precisely "to begin". Although it may seem simple and obvious, think about how long it took you to start reading and then to start following the suggested exercises. Let us think about how many excuses we have made for not continuing, even though we want to be happy or to improve the quality of our lives. The reasons why we might not really want to take this first step can be many. We may lack physical and mental strength, day-to-day inertia may be overwhelming, or we may be "too busy", stressed, or perhaps, we are even angry with ourselves or with the world. Anger generates a fierce inner tension that prevents us from seeing what is really happening to us. Being aware of these first pitfalls is the first big step and also the most important. In fact, coming to terms with the reality of our own status quo at the start of the journey is perhaps the most significant step forward on the path to happiness. When we finally decide to learn and to take action, the challenges of the different stages of the journey can also tempt us to abandon the quest along the way. How many times have we heard of people who have started a diet to lose weight but soon, for a variety of reasons, abandon the idea, sometimes causing a "rebound effect". This happens because the ground for making a success of a diet has not been properly prepared beforehand. People get fed up with self-imposed discipline when they are not psychologically ready for it, and of not seeing immediate results for their efforts. This can degenerate into a return to the rut of an unhealthy diet, and, in some cases because of disappointment and disillusion, there is even added weight gain.

Today, this "yo-yo" effect is a consequence not only of diets but also of many therapies. Society can demonstrate that many people tirelessly seek solutions for physical or mental imbalance in treatments or teachings of different kinds, obtaining scanty results despite the time and even money that might have been invested. We need to change our mental "chip". The process of learning to think correctly needs to be done in conjunction with PRACTICE. Wanting the whole project to be over with as quickly as possible is not a good sign. Following the necessary steps and enjoying the journey is much more hopeful. It is often the case when we start to retrain our minds that an imbalance of positive and negative ideas blurs the horizon. Do not give up. If we listen to ourselves a little and if we look deeper into ourselves, we can possibly see that this unsettling sensation is akin to that of being on the edge of a precipice looking down into a void. In fact, when a negative idea comes to mind, the most normal course of action would be to simply dispel it, which we can train ourselves to do. The reality is, however, that it is much easier to replace the negative idea with a positive one. Consequently, even if it has not disappeared entirely, the void will then shrink considerably. If we continue with the analysis, we may wonder where this sensation comes from when we try to keep negative thoughts and ideas out of mind. Did I not do the exercises correctly? Have I not been introspective enough? I want to rid myself of unhappiness and I have freely decided to do so, so what is happening to me? Why do I feel empty or even more miserable than before? When we think that we have a specific problem or many, it is most likely that we have carried them in our "backpack" for a long time, or at least it might seem that way. It has cost us a lot to feed our negative thinking day by day as if it were a small infant. Our mind was completely occupied doing just that. However, here and now we have decided to tread a new path and to get rid of our very own creation of negative thinking. This bubble of unhappiness, probably nurtured over many years like a parasitic growth, will already have mushroomed considerably and will probably be reproducing yet more negative ideas to complement the first. What happens to us at this stage of development as we are heading off on our newly chosen path? It may have cost us quite a lot of work, but finally, we have managed to replace those unproductive lines of thought with positive ones. However, the feeling of emptiness continues. Further analysis confirms that positive thinking can only ever be good for us, but of course, in this phase of our journey it is only a seed. There is still a way to go before we can talk of being completely happy.

It is likely that in the same way that a person can be addicted to alcohol, drugs or pleasure, we had become "hooked" on our negative ideology. It absorbed our energy and we spiralled into unhappiness. We had come to assume that the philosophy of being badly done by and that we had become one of life's victims was trapping us in a bubble of unreality, separate from the world and what it has to offer us. At this point, patience and perseverance must be our allies. Now is the time to nurture positive thinking, recreating ourselves through our new-found philosophy and pampering it as if it were a much-loved child. Later, when we externalise our new-found positivism, it will grow and with time, the emptiness that we felt at the beginning will only be a memory. Then, we can flourish. Retraining our mind, it gradually detaches itself from the negative; it "heals". Having replaced negative with positive, our being becomes more malleable, more creative, more orderly and less conflictive. Suddenly, our inner self connects with the world and with external reality. The things that happen to us begin to interact with each other and flow naturally. Now, the rest of the journey we undertake no longer costs us so much work, the stress disappears and so does the boredom. As we heal, the world around us also changes, but for the better. Finally, we become people of greater substance, grateful for everything we have in life and with more genuine desire to enjoy each day and to be more mindful of the needs of others. According to Buddhist tradition, there are three conflictive emotions or traits in humans that cause suffering and act as a barrier to happiness, i.e.

- anger and frustration;
- attachment to material possessions; and
- lack of consciousness or ignorance.

These are the precise negative features which could become obstacles along our road to happiness and get in the way of exercises and practices promoted in this book.

As I explained at the beginning of the book, when I was young, I learned a lot about Buddhist monks and their beliefs. I now want to finish this first and novel work of its kind with reference to them, thanking them for their teachings which set me out on the beginning of my own journey. The barriers that close the way to a full life are created by us, ourselves. It is in our hands to challenge this negativity. The results of our labours on this journey may vary, but we will, at the very least, have gained more knowledge about ourselves and others along the way. Our happiness is well worth the effort.

Chapter 12

Exercises

Next we will set out a series of exercises and practices that can help us to both relax and to concentrate more to tackle different situations of daily life. As indicated previously, they can be done at our convenience and according to the needs of the moment. This will give us a better base from which to concentrate more.

Exercise 1: <u>To secure more energy</u>

For this practice, you have to be calm, free from stress, alone in your room, on a comfortable sofa with your back straight, no noise, no music, no mobile phone, and you need to be sure you won't be interrupted for about 30 minutes. Breathe deeply and slowly for about two minutes. Concentrate on breathing. Now visualize in your mind a large white sphere, about 50 metres away from you. Observe how rays of white light, bright and charged with energy, emanate from this sphere. The sphere begins to move very slowly towards you.

Now you begin to notice how the rays impregnate you with a positive, relaxing energy. The closer it gets, the more you can feel its positive rays of energy. The sphere gets closer and closer to you to the point where it is touching you. It then gets smaller and smaller and then disappears. Stay about five minutes in your initial position, savouring these moments of total peace. Then, when you open your eyes, you will find yourself extremely relaxed, rested and charged with energy. The exercise can last between 30 and 45 minutes. If you can, repeat it about two days a week.

Exercise 2: <u>Practice to be more positive.</u>

Get used to doing this exercise in the mornings. After you have just got up, stand in front of the mirror and breathe deeply for a couple of minutes. Now fix your gaze onto the mirror and do the following: a few grimaces with your mouth using the muscles of your face. After about two minutes, pinch and squeeze your face with your fingertips for about two minutes. Now look again at your reflection in the mirror and say to yourself: "TODAY, EVERYTHING, absolutely everything will go well for me and no situation will keep me from feeling well and at ease with myself. Duration of exercise, 10 minutes. Try this three times a week.

Exercise 3: <u>Relaxation</u>

Sit on a chair or sofa with your back straight, eyes closed, no music, no noise, and your phone turned off. Make sure you are in a quiet place with the temperature just right and that you will not be disturbed for at least half an hour. Take about 12 deep breaths, inhaling the air through your nose, and expelling it very slowly through your mouth.

Between each inhalation, try to rest a short time without breathing, 10 or 20 seconds for example, as you prefer, but without forcing anything. Try to think about the breathing exercise and nothing else. If at any time an idea comes to your mind, just ignore it and it will disappear of its own accord. Now that you are calm, relaxed and comfortable, visualize a beautiful summer's day and imagine that you are on a beautiful beach in the Caribbean with crystal clear water in front of you. The environment is welcoming, warm and quiet with no one around. The sun is shining in all its splendour and power. You are now lying face-up by the sea in the sand, you feel how the gentle waves of sea water are caressing you. You feel the heat of the sand all over your body. Now close your eyes and take a deep breath. Everything is completely calm. The gentle movement of the waves engulfs you with its limitless energy. It is as if your whole body were a magnet that is being charged with the energy of the vast ocean. Enjoy this calm and tranquillity for about 30 minutes. Then open your eyes little by little and get up slowly. You will notice how well you feel and how relaxed you are. It is as if you had slept for 10 hours. Your whole body and mind feels completely at ease with itself.

Exercise 4: <u>Visualization for concentration</u>

Sit on a chair or sofa with your back straight, eyes closed, no music, no noise, your phone should be turned off and the room ideally needs to be at a pleasant temperature. Make sure that you are in a quiet place and that you will not be disturbed for at least half an hour. Now that you are relaxed and sitting quietly, visualize in your mind a huge, navy blue stone wall and that you are standing in front of it. Suddenly you see a hole in the wall. It is like a small entrance. You want to go through it because you see a tiny, bright white light on the other side. You try to get in through the hole, and you have to bend down a bit as the entrance is rather small. Once on the other side, you find yourself in a jungle which is wonderfully rich in plant life. You marvel at the beauty of its flora, majestic red and white plants amid a sea of lush green – all far removed from human habitation in a perfect climate. It is just like a miniature paradise with the sun shining high in the sky. Just in front of you, you can see a small path laid out with blue stones. You decide to follow the path, wondering where it will lead. After a few minutes, at the end of the trail, you come across a small wooden house with two white windows and a simple small door in the centre of the building. You enter the small cabin. There is only one tiny bed, also made of wood, and on top of it there is a white bedspread that covers the bed entirely. You lie down on the bed and notice how your body sinks a little into the soft mattress. You close your eyes and relax, enveloped by total tranquillity. The all-consuming peace brings with it a sense of complete harmony. Breathe gently and deeply for a couple of minutes. Feel how all your muscles are relaxing, notice a soft warmth engulfing your feet. This warmth rises to your arms and then on to your stomach and chest. Your mind and body are fully connected and at one in relaxation. In the distance you hear a cascade of crystalline water falling from a small spring. You can also hear very clearly the sweet song of the birds. It is like a soft melody that soothes you even more. It seems as if time has stood still for you, and that you are enjoying a great inner peace. Stay relaxed for about 15 minutes. You know that you can always return to this haven of peace whenever you wish. Now open your eyes and leave the small hut. Thank the jungle for its wonderful beauty and return to the wall along the same path from which you came. This exercise can last for about 55 minutes. It's alright if you fall asleep; that is a sign of being relaxed. Attempt the exercise two to three times a week. You will notice how after a few weeks, you feel better, without so much stress, and that you are able to concentrate more.

Exercise 5: <u>Gratitude and Forgiveness</u>

Sit in a chair or on a sofa with your back straight, eyes closed, no music, no noise and your mobile phone turned off. Make sure the room is at the right temperature for you and that it is a quiet space without disturbance for at least half an hour. Now that you are very relaxed and sitting quietly, practice remembering. Remember someone who gave you good news or who did something very positive for you. Visualize the moment in your mind. Then write the person's name and a thank-you message in your notebook acknowledging appreciation of what he or she did for you. Repeat this exercise at least two days a week.

Now try to remember someone who said or did something negative to you. Write their name in your notebook. Write a message saying that you forgive him or her for his or her actions. It doesn't matter if in both exercises the person concerned is no longer living. Don't avoid doing this exercise. You will witness the metamorphosis you undergo after a few weeks. You will feel a peace and tranquillity in your heart that did not exist before. A visualization session should come to an end gradually. First, the image is deliberately allowed to fade. Then slowly turn your attention back to the room in which you are sitting or lying, and then open your eyes. During the next few minutes, give your limbs a gentle stretch and then return to normal activity.

A finale, but without a farewell

During the reading of this book, we have walked together through twelve chapters. Now we have come to the end. I imagine there will have been varying degrees of acceptance of this work. It may have met your expect to a greater or lesser extent. It has been very interesting for me to accompany you in one way or another. The creation of "*Happiness in the 21st Century*" has transformed, for the better, my way of thinking and interacting with reality, and now I hope that I have done it for you, helped by communicating my life experiences. This is especially appropriate for those who have had "something" awakened in them through the reading of this book... an impulse, a real desire to move forward, and an urge to continue the work that they themselves have already begun. I would like then, to offer those who want it and/or feel that they need it, ongoing encouragement to boost your optimism. I can try to resolve any doubts you may have regarding the contents of the book. Within my

Manuel Sierra Jimenez

limitations, aided by common sense, I can give another "perspective" to questions that may arise when facing a varying range of problems within the framework of daily life. I would like to point out that the end of this reading is not a "farewell" and that in me, even at a distance, I remain a friend and above all someone who is willing to listen to you. If you want to contact me, you can do so through the following email: escipion555@hotmail.com.

Bibliography

The following books have been and are a great source of inspiration to me. Some of them I have read several times, and I am always surprised discovering new aspects in them. They have also provided me with valuable information when writing "HAPPINESS IN THE 21st CENTURY. Guide for a full life". For me, reading it is a reference point. I hope you will have the opportunity one day to read them. Without exaggerating, I can say that they are like food for the spirit.

WAYNE DYER: "The sky is the limit. Editorial Grijalbo (1980)

NAPOLEON HILL: "Think and become rich". Editorial Diamante (2014)

DANIEL GOLEMAN: "Emotional Intelligence". Editorial Kairos (1996)

WAYNE DYER: "Tus zonas erróneas". Editorial Casa del Libro (2010)

ROBIN S. SHARMA: "The monk who sold his ferrary". Editorial Grijalbo (2004)

OG MANDINO: "The biggest seller in the world". Editorial Grijalbo (1999)

KRISHNAMURTHI: "A los pies del maestro". Editorial Edaf (1997

KRISHNAMURTHI: "The mind in meditation". Editorial Kairos (2015)

RENÉ DESCARTES: "The discourse of the method". Editorial Akal (2007)

RENÉ DESCARTES: "Rules for the direction of the mind". Editorial Orbis (1983)

ROBERT KIYOSAKI and SHARON LECHTER: "Padre Rico Padre Pobre". Editorial Aguilar (2008) CONFUCIO: "I-ching, el libro de las Mutaciones". Editorial Edhara (1990)

FRIEDRICH NIETZSCHE: "Thus spoke Zarathustra". Editorial Euroliber (1994)

JOAN MASCARÓ and R. CRESPO (translators): "Los Upanishads". Editorial Diana (1976)

DALE CARNEGIE: "How to speak well in public and influir in business". Editorial Cosmos (2008) DALE CARNEGIE: "Cómo ganar amigos e influir sobre las personas". Editorial Edhasa (1983) RONDA BYRME: "The secret". Editorial Urano (2012)

FRIEDRICH NIETZSCHE: "Beyond good and evil". Editorial Orbis (1983)

ADAM J. JACKSON: "The Ten Secrets of Abundant Wealth". Editorial Sirio (1962)

GABRIEL GARCÍA MÁRQUEZ: "One hundred years of solitude". Editorial Edhasa (1967)

PAULO COELHO: "The Alchemist". Editorial Planeta (1997)

PAULO COELHO: "El Zahir". Editorial Planeta (2005)

CONNY MÉNDEZ: "Metaphysics within everyone's reach". Editorial Giluz (2017)

SAINT GERMAIN: "Yo soy, la mágica presencia". Editorial Humanitas (2005)

SAINT GERMAIN: "El séptimo rayo". Editorial Humanitas (1990)

SAINT GERMAIN: "Misterios desvelados". Editorial Humanitas (2010)

PATANJALI: "Yoga sutras". Editorial Synchrony (2016)

ERICH FROMM: "The art of loving". Editorial Paidos (1973)

FRANCESC MIRALLES and HÉCTOR GARCÍA: "The secrets of Japan for a long and happy life.

About the Author

Manuel Sierra Jimenez, born in Badajoz in southern Spain in 1965, moved to the Balearic Islands with his family when he was a child but not before recovering from what appeared to be permanent paralysis through an inexplicable cure. Discriminated against as an "outsider" during his school days on Mallorca, his life was revolutionised after a meeting with a visiting group of Tibetan monks. Self-help, the search for a deeper meaning to our existence and a desire to bring out the fullness of life for all us underpins Manuel's foray into Buddhism and alternative ways of looking at the world.